Shakespeare at My Shoulder

Other books and plays by the Johnsons:

Drama for Classroom and Stage
Directing Methods
Drama for Junior High
Shakespeare Vignettes
Oral Reading: Creative and Interpretive
To See a Play
Plays for Readers' Theatre
Church Plays and How to Stage Them
Best Church Plays
Adam and Eve Meet the Atom
Even the Hater
The People versus Christ
The Innocent
We Give You Gilbert and Sullivan

Albert Johnson,

Shakespeare at My Shoulder

Albert and Bertha Johnson

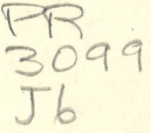

PR
3099
J6

South Brunswick and New York: A. S. Barnes and Co.
London: Thomas Yoseloff Ltd

© 1972 by A. S. Barnes and Co., Inc.

A. S. Barnes and Co., Inc.
Cranbury, New Jersey 08512

Thomas Yoseloff Ltd
108 New Bond Street
London W1Y OQX, England

Library of Congress Cataloging in Publication Data

Johnson, Albert.
  Shakespeare at my shoulder.

  1. Shakespeare, William, 1564–1616—Stage history—1800.
I. Johnson, Bertha, joint author. II. Title.
PR3099.J6   822.3'3   73-37829
ISBN 0-498-01106-2

Printed in the United States of America

This book is gratefully and lovingly dedicated
to Caroline Mattingly Prendergast,
who first inspired our love affair with Shakespeare

Contents

Prologue		9
1	Farce Is More Than Funny Business	27
	The Taming of the Shrew—Directing Concept	37
2	To Tell Again of Shylock and Fair Portia	41
	The Merchant of Venice—Directing Concept	45
3	Of Lovers, Artisans, and Sprites	55
	A Midsummer Night's Dream—Directing Concept	59
4	When Witches Work Their Evil Spell	63
	The Tragedy of Macbeth—Directing Concept	70
5	Spirits Who Lift the Soul to Light	72
	The Tempest—Directing Concept	77
6	Two Viewpoints on the Danish Prince	82
	Hamlet, Prince of Denmark—Directing Concept One	84
	Hamlet, Prince of Denmark—Directing Concept Two	87
7	What Light from Yonder Window Breaks?	95
	Romeo and Juliet—Directing Concept	102
8	From Stage to Camera with the Bard	111
9	Genius: Genes or Hard Knocks?	126

Prologue

The bust of William Shakespeare cannot speak. With serene expression it graces the study shelf in silence. Yet in that silence there is a presence which anyone who tampers with his plays is likely to sense. Not from the plaster image of the man, but from his immortal words the presence springs. Friend or foe, this presence? Hexing haunt, or helpful spirit?

Rewriting Shakespeare had better be no arrogant ego trip. If so, the hex! But earnest, agonizing faithfulness to Will's intent seems to bring his benison. One needs his blessing, needs it badly when called upon to shape his plays to modern stage and television tube. One works, or one had darned well better work, not in the shadow of the specter, but in the light of the spirit. Efforts to do so are rewarding, and the rewards take voice and cry out to be shared.

Discoveries made in the editing of Shakespeare's plays for stage and television are too germane to the current human crisis not to be shared. Can that genius of the seventeenth century solve the problems of the late twentieth? Perhaps not, but a fresh perspective on the works of that genius cannot fail to spark new prospects.

To live through the years with the people of Shakespeare's plays is an experience we Johnsons yearn to extend to others. The essence of that experience is, we believe, adumbrated in the directing concepts around which the content of this book is centered. Our directing concepts, first written for the casts of the seven plays selected, were later shared with playgoers, many of whom have encouraged their publication. That encouragement has led to their expansion, in the hope of enriching the pleasure of play readers as well as playgoers, and with the more important hope that many who have neither read nor seen the plays of William Shakespeare will feel impelled to fill that cultural gap.

It is not only to directors, designers, actors, and students of drama and theatre arts that we address these pages. What we are saying may be of professional significance to them. To others, however, particularly playgoers, readers of plays, English teachers, and Shakespearephiles, the book may serve as passport to new vistas in familiar country. The concepts and accompanying comments will, it is hoped, provoke fresh insight into the genius of Shakespeare and the immortal works of that genius.

Directors will know at once what is meant by a directing concept. To others the term may need some explanation. In essence, the term is merely the viewpoint of the person who is staging the play. Every director has a viewpoint, a position, a posture, a general concept, even though that concept is often not set down on paper. He, the director, knows what he wants the play to say, and in forming that opinion, he usually hews to the line of what the playwright means to say, or at least to what he believes the playwright means to say. There are, there always have been, directors who take a virtuoso approach and deliberately shape the play into something not intended by the author, but even such a cavalier approach amounts to a viewpoint or a concept.

Each of the seven plays for which we present directing concepts is a touchstone for ideas and relevant reminiscences, which will be followed in chapter 8 with a close-up view of how a play gets transferred from stage to television screen. In the final chapter we shall explore the genius itself, that genius which was Shakespeare. How does a Shakespeare get to be a Shakespeare? Is there a formula for genius? How does one account for those giant souls who walk the earth once or twice in a thousand years? The exploration invites adventure.

Theatre buffs and Shakespeare fans may be with us or leaping ahead at this point. If they will patiently stand by for a slight detour, we want to travel the high school route for a moment. Hundreds of thousands of high school students study the plays of William Shakespeare in their English courses. What can we say to them and to their teachers? What we do say, we hope, will save many a student from being turned off, as thousands are each year, for want of a stimulating and exciting approach to one of the greatest minds of all time. The turn-off is even more dreadful when we consider what Shakespeare means to the civilized world. He is to the literate world what Darwin, Freud, and Einstein are to the world of science.

When we consider the impact that Shakespeare has had and continues to have on the civilized world, we realize that to shortchange our young people in acquainting them with him is to deny them an inalienable right. At a time when the young, and some older people as well, are groping for new values, a fresh view of Shakespeare's plays and the remarkable people of those plays seems especially pertinent. Radical ideas are in the air. Conventions are challenged. Traditions are toppled. It is incumbent on our changing world to reexplore the world of Shakespeare. One way of reexploration is through directing concepts.

Certainly some of the most fascinating characters ever created leap at us from the pages of Shakespeare's plays to breathe and live on the living stage. Getting to know those characters, living with them through all their incredible imbroglios, coming to care about them as people can hardly be anything short of stimulating and challenging. To see those people in a freshly filtered light, moving to a different drum beat, projecting themselves into contemporary thought—such is the avowed purpose of our directing concepts.

To deprive young people of one of the richest treasures of their heritage seems culturally criminal. Yet many are deprived, some by a popular misapprehension that Shakespeare is, to use that current hackneyed phrase, "not relevant." Not relevant! Not relevant to what? Any notion that he is not relevant to the richest possible fulfillment of life must certainly be due to some dull, pedagogical misrepresentation of the Bard. Teachers who are ill-prepared can cause a lot of mischief, and that mischief is visited on the unfortunate generations. The friendly ghost of gentle Will urges that we try to remedy such mischief. To meet the mischief problem head-on, a question or two will serve as cue.

Why is Shakespeare taught in high school? Why is Shakespeare taught in college and university? Why are his plays performed in thousands of cities all over the world? *Hamlet* in Japanese, *Macbeth* in German, *Othello* in Italian, and *Romeo and Juliet* in modern Greek! Why are there so many theatrical companies devoted primarily, or even exclusively, to the presentation of Shakespearean plays? This sort of thing has been going on for nearly four hundred years. Why? Why, especially, is Shakespeare so popular in contemporary times? Why is it that, for many generations, Shakespeare has been second in popularity only to the Bible throughout the English-speaking world?

A bit of pondering on such questions should bring our proposition into focus. Educated people throughout the civilized world know something about Shakespeare. Even people with limited formal education feel the magnitude of his titanic talent. After all, he wrote for the groundlings quite as much as for the aristocracy seated in the galleries, and the groundlings of today flock to his plays, particularly when many are students obliged to bargain for the cheapest seats.

One need not be a Ph.D. to feel and show the influence of that poet-dramatist. His words are heard among the lowly and the learned. Consider, for example, the following random quotations, and the diversity of people who are likely to use them:

"My kingdom for a horse . . ."

"I come to bury Caesar, not to praise him . . ."

"The fault, dear Brutus . . ."

"All the world's a stage . . ."

"Hold the mirror up to nature . . ."

"To thine own self be true . . ."

"The quality of mercy is not strained . . ."

"Now I am alone . . ."

"To be or not to be . . ."

"Out, damned spot. . . ."

Many of these phrases have become clichés and platitudes, commonly spoken by common people in common places, often with no awareness of the source. No credits, no residuals for poor Will. Yet our language has been eternally enriched by his plays and poems, which, incidentally, are not generally rejected by our counter-culture group. Given a decent exposure to Shakespeare, the kids dig him. For most of them, that giant of the Renaissance transcends the challenge of the Establishment. We should not be surprised at this, since he has transcended all other revolutions. For centuries Shakespeare has been power to the people, though not to those who have suffered a power shortage due to some disastrous short circuit in pedagogical imagination.

It may be that our newly enlightened youth have discovered something that their elders have forgotten or never knew, which is that Shakespeare did not write for English courses, or for professors absorbed with sources, symbolism, and versification, or for scholars hunting and pecking their way to the Ph.D. He didn't even write for posterity.

There seems little evidence that he gave a second thought to what future generations would think about his plays. Knowing that the theatre is ephemeral by its very nature, he wanted to reach the playgoers of his time *there,* in a limited patch of England. There is also little evidence that he labored excessively to create the greatest poetry in the world. He was a poet and a poet writes poetry. He was a genius too, but it isn't likely that he thought of himself as anything special or unusual. On the contrary, he may have felt his lack of college training a serious handicap in competition with such university men as Ben Jonson and Christopher Marlowe. He was primarily a playwright writing for the stage.

Writing for the stage in any age means writing under pressure. Any thought of a Shakespeare taking years, or even months, to compose a masterpiece in some remote, halcyon haven to the idyllic chirping of birds is probably pure romantic fantasy. It is much more likely that he scrawled his plays out, scene by scene, sweating or shivering in some noisy alehouse between performances. Dialogue that didn't sound right in rehearsal had to be rewritten, scenes had to be revised, action altered, and always there was the deadline of that final rehearsal. Certainly he was no hack writer, but he must often have had to work as though he were one.

To some, the recognition of these facts may seem like a heretical put-down. It will not seem so to those who know what it is to write for the theatre. On the contrary, such a flow of brilliant and beautiful words under such conditions is the greatest possible evidence of genius.

Since this is not a biography of William Shakespeare or a history of his time, we can dispense with much material that has been dealt with interestingly and exhaustively elsewhere. Here we are concerned with that specter at the shoulder, that ghostly breath that chills the neck. That bust up there on the study shelf looks down. What are we doing to his plays? What have the countless actors, producers, critics, and doctoral candidates done through the centuries? The gaze of the bust is passive, unruffled, undisturbed. What they have done and what we have done are but pygmy pickings in enduring granite. We chisel, scratch, and alter, but cannot move the mountain. Always, in the end, the mountain wins. We, like Mohammed, must go to it.

We Johnsons have produced many of Shakespeare's plays, some many times, yet each production has been different from all others. For example, we have presented several versions of *Hamlet*. Each time, our directing concept has been different. Ergo, each time, we have altered the text, cutting segments of the play, deleting lines, rearranging the sequence of the scenes, yet, no matter how we change the text, the play transcends the alterations. Truncate and alter as we will, *Hamlet* still comes out as *Hamlet*. That is the hallmark of genius. That is the test of the greatness of a play.

Is this to argue that Shakespeare's plays cannot be killed? No, that is not our argument. His plays, like any others, can be mutilated and totally distorted from what the author had in mind. Such things can happen, have happened, do happen, and we have witnessed such insults, but we avow that a play by William Shakespeare cannot be killed unless there is a deliberate intent to do so. Directors who try honestly to project the author's intent will almost always find that the play survives their careful modifications.

"The author's intent." This brings us back to that haunting, hounding specter at the shoulder. Haunt us, gentle Will!

We who love the plays of Shakespeare love them in text as well as in production. There are even those who prefer the text to the staging of the play. They would rather read than view a play. They argue that to read the play enables them to envision in their own minds the many marvelous worlds the words connote. They would rather imagine than behold, would rather hear in the mind's ear the sound and music implicit in the text. For them, the directing concepts in the following pages may serve as prologue to their next rereading of the plays, and may, as program notes often do at a musical recital or at a symphony concert, embellish their enjoyment. Such notes in the form of directing concepts should whet the imagination, which is the gateway to the garden of enjoyment.

For those who like to see and hear the plays in living action, the directing concepts will have a slightly different value. The concepts may be prologue and program notes to them as well, but with some added challenge. Playgoers with an idée fixe about the way the play should look and sound may be stimulated by ideas that seem radically disturbing. Bueno, bien, sehr gut! To stimulate and challenge is certainly one of our objectives. In fact, that is always the purpose of a directing concept.

The director asks himself: What is this play about? What is the theme? What is the premise, the proposition, or, if you will, the moral? Who is the protagonist, the central character, the lead? What is his problem, his goal, his objective; what is it that he wants? Why can't he have it? Who and what blocks him from reaching his goal? What is he like, this protagonist? Or we might well say, what is she like? There are some feminine protagonists. What makes her or him tick? What are the other characters like? What makes each of them tick? Such questions and many more go through the director's mind as he does his homework on the play he is to produce.

His concept will include, in addition to character analysis, his idea of how the play should be staged. He makes a choice between a simple or an elaborate method of staging. He must decide about the scenery, the lighting, the costuming, and the sound and music.

To all these things he must add mood and dramatic style, and then contrive to clarify them for his actors and his crews. This he does sometimes with words set on paper, words rarely seen by people outside the acting company. Sometimes his words are tersely stated in a paragraph or two, sometimes they take the form of essays. The statement or the essay may use implication or be direct. In many cases words do not get to paper ever, but reach the actors by word of mouth in rehearsals, conferences, and rap sessions.

In general, it is safe to say that there are as many directing concepts as there are directors. This is especially true with the plays of Shakespeare. Again it is a tribute to his genius that he could create a play for a bare stage of the Elizabethan theatre that can be done so many different ways. In the past three hundred years, the plays of William Shakespeare have been presented in every conceivable way. No. Let us correct that statement. Not every conceivable way. New ways of staging Shakespeare are constantly being conceived, to wit, Peter Brooks' recent production of *A Midsummer Night's Dream,* Peter Hall's *Macbeth* at Stratford-on-Avon, and Richard Chamberlain's unconventional *Hamlet.* The infinite variety of ways in which his plays can be produced should serve to pique our interest in any new directing concept of a Shakespearean play.

An added fascination for directors may be the reminder of how directors borrow from one another. Rarely does a director try to lift a directing concept as an out-and-out act of plagiarism. Actually, such an attempt would prove disillusioning, because no one can duplicate the spirit of another person's production. It is the legitimate borrowing that is worthy of attention.

Margaret Webster, the famous British Shakespearean producer, liked our simple rolling scenery unit, which we used in one of our early productions of *Hamlet.* Upon seeing our production, she went home to design something quite similar for her production of *The Tempest.*

In turn, directors all through England and America have

borrowed ideas from the concepts so lucidly articulated in Miss Webster's book *Shakespeare without Tears*. Curiously, a concept of one play may serve to spark a concept for a totally different play. Ideas from a Birmingham Repertory treatment of *As You Like It* surfaced in our concept of *The Tempest,* and the Old Vic concept of *Romeo and Juliet* furnished a transfusion for our production of that play.

While most directors believe that the basic inspiration for a directing concept has to come from the text itself, all are surely aware of contributing, collateral influence. More than most playrights, Shakespeare sends us to our reference shelves, sets us to scanning the famous Variorum edition, and alerts us in general to any and all sources of ideas. Certainly to read about a play is no substitute for an intensive study of the play itself, but what critics and other directors have said or written often meshes fruitfully with the creative imagination.

Actors, too, accept the text as their bench mark. An actor begins by reading the play through many times. He cannot thoroughly understand his role until he sees it in juxtaposition to all the other roles. An actor who goes charging off in singular pursuit of his part in the play, with no consideration of who his character is in relation to the plot and other characters, is like a soloist who is unmindful of conductor or accompaniment. A good actor studies the play and then his role, drinking deeply from the springs of the text.

Yet actors, like directors, welcome all the help they can get from complementary sources. It is the function of the directing concept to give the actors just such help. If the concept is clearly articulated, it gives the actors a sense of direction. The objective of the play and their individual objectives in the play are implied if not defined. They sense their common goal and find it exciting to grow together. Once they grasp the content of the concept, they feel they are in orbit, shooting on target.

A study of their director's concept also helps the actors to play together. Like rap sessions, which are always a suitable corollary, it makes for good ensemble playing. In the long soul-searching quest for the soul of a character, an actor can become very lonely. Guidelines from the concept help him find his identity, while at the same time those same guidelines are helping his fellow players.

Reading, and particularly rereading a directing concept, often throws a light beam into hitherto shadowed areas. Portions of the text that may have been obscure suddenly come into focus. A highlight on scene six makes something in scene three make sense. Merely a subtle reference to a line, a relationship, or a bit of business may suddenly give relevance to something that had seemed woefully unrelated. So aided, the actors feel much less handicapped in their effort to get it all together. Such are the ends the directing concept should serve.

With the shadow of the immortal Will still at the shoulder, we seek to guide that laser beam which is his spirit to a burning away of the murkiness that seems to fog imagination. We, like millions of others, are disturbed by a growing awareness of that murkiness. Something is dulling the luster of the human mind. Technology, politics, war, repression, revolution? Who knows? We do know that we cannot go back to some blossom-scented Eden. The age of innocence is lost to all of us, but in those worlds which Shakespeare wakens, we may find gardens yet unexplored and promises of marvels still undreamed of.

So let us get to know those fascinating, three-dimensional

characters of Shakespeare's plays. No one who really gets to know them is ever turned off by Shakespeare. Nowhere in all the literature of the world are we likely to meet such people. They are people of such depth, breadth, stature, and diverse psychological characteristics that we can never know them all, or even know all about any one of them, all of which adds to the fathomless depths of the genius who created them. We cannot know them all, or thoroughly, but that is no good reason for not trying to know them better, for the truth is, the better we know them, the better we may come to know our neighbors and ourselves.

Gather round and let us think about the thoughts that flash through the minds of those Shakespearean characters. There are high thoughts and base ones, thoughts heroic and thoughts villainous. There are thoughts and deeds of tenderness, and thoughts and deeds of violence. There is meanness, depravity, utter baseness, and there is compassion and transcending glory. Do let us think about the thoughts of that incredible provoker of thought.

Let us think too about the power and the beauty of the language of the plays. Even when we delete those passages which may have made sense to the Elizabethans but are obscure and dull to us, even, or perhaps especially, when that is done, the language is a symphony of sound. Beethoven with all his themes, Mozart with his fresh and memorable melodies, Bach with his counterpoint—they all did with music what Shakespeare did with words.

With such a wealth of words available, one wonders how there can be so many people who are grounded by limited vocabularies; there are even those who are content to communicate, if it be communication, with grunts and snorts and monosyllabic utterances. And all the while there is that vibrant, resonant, dynamic language of Will Shakespeare sounding in the winds for those who will to hear.

Shakespeare wrote for his audience in his theatre in his time. What about directors who have to produce his plays for audiences of their time?

That question was put to us by a friend who, like many a playgoer, wonders how playwright, director, and actors ever get together on the interpretation of a play. As our friend points out, the author has his own ideas; the director, who usually feels aesthetically bound to be true to the author's intent, has his; and the actors, if they are not mere puppets, certainly have theirs. The outcome, one might guess, might be utter chaos. So it might. So it sometimes is. A strong preventative is the directing concept.

The concept, being a statement of the director's intent, becomes the frame of reference. Although it is neither manifesto nor holy writ, it is a basic point of view which is presented to the cast on an open-ended basis. Discussion ensues, ideas fly back and forth, character insights are explored, dramatic values examined. Actors talk. Directors listen. The feedback is evaluated, and the concept is clarified and confirmed, invariably enriched by the contributions of the actors, who, with the director, now know what beat they're on and where they're headed. They may be blown off course from time to time, may even explore intriguing detours, but with the concept as chart, the director at the helm can always tack back on course.

The director's hassle with the playwright is another matter. If the playwright is alive and well, providing problems with his propinquity, the matter may indeed become a hassle. Hassles, however, can be fruitful. Out of healthy disagreement can come new, mutual understanding, particularly when the disagreeing parties disagree agreeably. The author is creator, the director is interpreter, though each may find himself interpreting and creating in the meeting of their minds, and in the borning of the play. So much for hammering out a concept for a product of a living playwright.

Suppose the playwright is not alive and well, and there is no problem of propinquity. What then? No problem? Guess again. No director, even though he be totally free of superstition, can be altogether comfortable about that matter of propinquity. No director, did we say? Perhaps that's not quite true. The many mutilations of Shakespearean plays suggest that the potential presence of the haunting bard has not always pricked at consciences. Probably there have been enough mutilations of some of Shakespeare's plays to turn—if the dead can really roll over in their graves—the buried body of the bard into a whirling dervish.

All through the nineteenth century there were actor-managers who did incredible things to Shakespearean texts. Stars, they called themselves, catering to audiences they believed came more to see them than to see the play. They tailored text to acting ego, fattening their parts to the diminishing of other roles, twisting the plots, altering the dialogue, and distorting the very meaning of the play. Pirates they were, plowing the seas of the public domain. With them the play decidedly was not the thing.

In contrast to those nineteenth-century four-flushers were the faithful followers of the Shakespeare texts in such theatres as England's Old Vic, where directors often went to the other extreme. Benefiting from the wealth of scholarship and recent research, Old Vic directors often produced texts in their entirety, resulting in performances that lasted from three to five hours. Such reverence for pure Shakespeare meant the inclusion of passages that were obscure to modern audiences, but Old Vic actors were trained to make even the obscure make sense.

Unfortunately, all actors are not so trained, and audiences are not presently inclined to favor five-hour shows or sit with patience through archaic passages and obscure dialogue. The contemporary playgoer welcomes fidelity to the text so long as that fidelity does not interfere with the entertaining power of the play. He, like the playgoers of Shakespeare's time, wants entertainment, and entertainment is what Will himself was dedicated to provide. The play may carry a message, may edify, may inspire, may ridicule or satirize, may quicken the mind or sicken the heart, but it must entertain. So Will believed. So we believe.

On that assumption we proceed, hoping that what we have to say about the seven plays we have chosen to discuss will add enchantment and enlightenment to entertainment. From the various Shakespearean plays we have produced, we have selected seven on which to make our directorial comments. The seven are *The Taming of the Shrew, The Merchant of Venice, A Midsummer Night's Dream, The Tempest, Macbeth, Hamlet,* and *Romeo and Juliet.*

Our directing concepts of these seven have been shared before with audiences as well as actors, and—with that ever-faithful bust still watching from the shelf—we have since edited for whom it may concern.

Shakespeare at My Shoulder

1
Farce Is More Than Funny Business

We begin our directing concepts with *The Taming of the Shrew,* one of Shakespeare's few farces, and one of the funniest of his plays. To some, the fact that it is funny might make it seem easy to produce. The opposite is true. What appears funny on the page is funny on the stage only when it is clearly conceived and carefully rehearsed. Of all dramatic forms, farce is the most difficult to stage with finesse, and if it lacks finesse, it invariably falls flat.

One reason for this is that in farce we are dealing with highly improbable, though entirely possible, situations. There must be a fine balance between the ridiculous and the plausible. It is the happy acceptance of absurdities that delights the audience.

What is true of situations is equally true of the characters. There is always the temptation to exaggerate the characters, to push them beyond the point of credibility; in short, to turn them into caricatures. To yield to such a temptation is disastrous. Ridiculous as they may appear at times, the characters must be thoroughly believable. They are amusing only so long as we believe in their make-believe.

Another thing that makes farce difficult to produce is

Katharine and Petruchio, *The Taming of the Shrew*

the intricate stage business which is invariably called for. There should be funny business in abundance, but never funny business merely for the sake of funny business. It must be motivated, which is to say it should be something that we might reasonably expect the characters to do. When Hortensio runs on with a lute smashed over his head, we know at once that the impetuous shrew has conked him during the music lesson. When Petruchio picks up the defiant Kate and tosses her over his shoulder for a flamboyant exit, the business must appear as inevitable as it is impetuous.

Another point is the timing. In the first place, each bit of pantomine must be worked out in great detail and then rehearsed meticulously. In farce, the timing is everything. Farce is a style that calls for great precision. The use of the innumerable props in the supper scene and in the subsequent tailor scene in Petruchio's house is an excellent example of situations where precision is called for.

Because Shakespeare's texts provide only the sketchiest of hints to suggest any stage business, directors have to be highly inventive, though some invention can be, and often is, left to the actors. Through the years much tradition has been accumulated and passed along from generation to generation, but even so, directors usually like to allow themselves plenty of room for invention.

There is, of course, much more to farce than well-timed action. There is, above all, the comment. All the fun must add up to something. There should be more to the play than froth and frosting. Out of the fun comes the sum and substance of the author's comment. Here is where the director needs the playwright at his shoulder. Here, even more than in textual editing, the director gropes for the author's intent.

The groping, which is rarely in vain, reaps varying rewards. We have produced *The Taming of the Shrew* many times, and always with a slightly different concept, yet have

The Tailor scene, *The Taming of the Shrew*

always been faithful (at least in our fashion) to Shakespeare's intent.

If our concept of the play differs from yours it will not mean that we are right and you are wrong, or vice versa. Rather, it only indicates again the vastness of a talent that can inspire an infinite variety of reactions. This concept like all the ensuing ones, is an invitation to your imagination. You are invited to share our pleasure in the preparation of plays for production. To us, it seems a pleasure too rare to file or shelve.

Ideally, we should love to take our readers through the total experience of each production preparation, but that would be a process that evades description. Furthermore, there would be pangs and pains to mar the pleasure. Productions are always fraught with problems, problems which fortunately the audience is never aware of. Playgoers pay their admissions to see plays, and not to share the headaches of the producers. So it is our mission here to share the ecstacy without the agony, the fun without the fury, the entertainment without the hassle of getting the play produced.

One hope we have is that you will come to care for the plays and the people of the plays as we have come to love them. Perhaps it is familiarity that has fed our fondness. Living with those characters day and night, as we do when in production, we come to think of them as family.

They are like members of a successful commune. We get to know them intimately.

Petruchio, we soon discover, is something more than a "mad-brain rudesby, full of spleen," and the fiery, sexy Katharine much more than "an irksome, brawling scold." Bianca, spoiled brat that she is, has charm quite irresistible, and poor old Papa Baptista has problems we quickly care to share. Then there is that lovable clown of a Grumio, taking the curses and the blows of his master, Petruchio,

Bianca and her suitors, *The Taming of the Shrew*

playing the dolt, yet clearly in on the mischief-making of his master, and making mischief of his own abetted by that motley bevy of domestics who plot to give Kate a rough time. Those domestics, too, like all the suitors and all the other characters who dash in and out, are fascinating people. All of them will win our hearts before we're half way to the opening night.

How can we feel at home with the coarseness and brutality of such people? Coarse? Brutal? Petruchio and Kate? Oh, yes, we know some see them so. Some see *The Taming of the Shrew* as a bestial clash of uncontrollable temper with intolerable violence, but as we get to know these people, we find much more humanity than such a viewpoint would allow. It is a war of wits, not weapons. The comedy lies not in brutal beatings, which is never laugh material on a level higher than moronic adolescence, but in the clash of witty minds, and minds at work are much more fun to watch than crude bludgeonings. A temper tamed with club or fist does not stay tamed but only cowed. Such things we learn from characters who will assert themselves when given half a chance. On the page those Shakespearean characters may seem fictional, but give them tights and farthingales and they begin to breathe.

Actually, the breathing begins long before they go to wardrobe. Actors breathe well, and have a way of giving voice to breath, and often thought to voice. Suddenly we are with Grumio, Hortensio, Bianca, and Baptista. When we came in they were actors huddling over scripts. Then, there before our eyes, in presence of our listening ears, they turn into dramatis personae, and they are teaching us how they should sound and look.

"Verona for a while I take my leave." It is Petruchio speaking now, not just the actor. "They call me Katharine that do speak of me." It is indeed a Katharine speaking.

"You lie, in faith; for you are call'd plain Kate." Petruchio again. "The prettiest Kate in Christendom."

"Let him that moved thee hither, remove you hence." The fire is lit. The fictional figures are now warm flesh

Katharine, *The Taming of the Shrew*

and blood. The book's page becomes the stage. They leap from the text, those characters, leap pell-mell into life, and life with them, we know at once, cannot be anything but lively.

They will teach us by the very lines that Shakespeare wrote that this is more than slapstick farce. Horseplay there is, and horseplay aplenty along the way "to kill a wife with kindness," but all the nonsense must make sense if Shakespeare is to be allowed to make his point. That point is in the very make-up of the heroine Kate, and she must give us hints of what she really is behind the masquerade of temper and defiance. Time and again we must see shrewdness beneath that shrewishness.

We must see clearly from the start that what she wants is what she gets, outfoxing her braggart of a husband in the process. We must know too that what Petruchio says he wants, he wants—that Kate shall be his wife. He'll nag, he'll tantalize, he'll tease, but in the end he'll beam with pride and joy to have the Katharine that has turned the tables on his taming.

Although Kate is rocked back on her haunches for a while when she has met her match, her turnabout in her final scene—beautifully prepared for in the preceding scene on the way to her father's house (the famous sun and moon scene)—delivers in delectable satire Shakespeare's point.

In mock acceptance of her modest, feminine role, she spoofs all women, while at the same time ribbing male chauvinism in a manner that would win her Brownie points with Women's Lib.

"I am ashamed that women are so simple to offer war where they should kneel for peace." What she does with that word "simple" and with a glance at Petruchio asserts that her irony is not lost on her husband.

"Or seek for rule, supremacy and sway when they are bound to serve, love, and obey." She is kidding the women. She is pulling their legs, especially with those last three words "serve, love, obey." At the same time her eyes are

Bianca, *The Taming of the Shrew*

flashing to Petruchio a sign that could be either victory or peace!

The Taming of the Shrew
DIRECTING CONCEPT

When a cocky, self-confident bronco buster tackles a spirited, unbridled filly, a rollicking imbroglio is certain to result. Braggart boy meets haughty girl and Cupid's darts are suddenly high voltage. This is a game that must be played for keeps, for Kate cannot be tamed until she's won, and can't be won by he-man prowess purely.

Petruchio is out to "wive and thrive as best he can." Why came he hither but to that intent? The proud, disdainful Katharine will not be Bianca-bait to be auctioned off to the first bidder just so her beautiful, pampered brat of a sister can have her choice of suitors. She'll marry whom and when she pleases, and when she does she'll not be quick to veil her stubborn pride. It will be wit for wit and tongue for tongue until she sees it is her pride and not her will her man would conquer.

Wild as the world is in Kate's new home, it is a world of Petruchio's invention and the farcical, frenetic folderol is but a game to tame a dame. This is a war of the wills and wits and words. Wills that will not be broken, wits that clash in the sheer joy of an intellectual joust, words that flash like sparks from foils, but they are foils, not rapiers.

The fencing is for fun, not blood. The touch is but to bring her from a wild Kate to a "Kate conformable." Yet not too literally "like other household Kates." Petruchio could never live with groveling conformity, and Kate

Katharine and Petruchio, *The Taming of the Shrew*

would not be Kate by catering to his every whim without the inward triumph of her own incomparable whimsy.

Wearying for an instant with the game that gets him nowhere, Petruchio will drop his punitive pursuit to try sweet reason. Kate will thrust, not with a thunderous jolt, but with a gesture. Then in the light of moon, or sun, or whatever he may choose to call it, Kate calls the play and

Katharine and Petruchio, *The Taming of the Shrew*

the game is hers. Now she will play it to the gallery, a show to amuse her husband and to amaze all others.

Here is a wonder, if you ask for a wonder, and the wonder is one the world has yet to find, for the wonder is that the gesture does what force can never do. The gesture, if it be in faith, in love, and with a sense of humor, can bring about negotiated peace.

Here is a wonder, a gesture, a play, but most of all, a play. What does it say? HUMBLE YOUR PRIDE. SHE WHO WILL CONQUER WILL HAVE THE WIT TO BOW. PRIDE PERPETUATES PROSECUTION. HUMILITY HERALDS GOOD WILL.

Here, between decorated Italian pillars, in a blaze of color, is the risible, riotous Renaissance. It is song, it is laughter, it is noise. It is the sound of the Renaissance in the key of comedy in a lively allegretto. It is the Renaissance of long ago, likewise the renaissance of now. For men still try to tame, and there are shrews who choose to call the sun the sun—even in this, our age of new enlightenment.

2
To Tell Again of Shylock and Fair Portia

"In Belmont is a lady richly left; and she is fair, and fairer than that word of wondrous virtue. . . . Nor is the wide world ignorant of her worth, for the fourwinds blow in from every coast renowned suitors, and her sunny locks hang on her temples like a golden fleece, which makes her seat of Belmont Colchos' strand, and many Jasons come in quest of her."

With such poetic words does the enamoured Bassanio launch a chain reaction that makes *The Merchant of Venice* one of Shakespeare's most popular plays.

The lady, of course, is Portia, a witty, capricious cut-up whose capacity to rise to noble heights is more than match to her mischievous flirtations. Portia, the role that every actress and likely every high school girl has pined to play! How many youngsters through the years have tried alone before their mirrors, "The quality of mercy is not strained; it droppeth as the gentle rain from Heaven"?

Portia is and has been through the centuries the coveted

prize of nearly every actress great and small. No wonder, when we remember how the fun-loving belle of Belmont ripens into full, self-confident womanhood when she finds her true love and finds him in dire trouble.

Shylock, too, has had his share of aspirants. "Three thousand ducats. 'Tis a good round sum." How many lads have tried those lines, trying to sound like Shylock? The number could be counted as a good round sum, no doubt.

The stage history of Shylock is as varied as it is fascinating. Actors playing Shylock through the centuries have run the gamut from comic role to tragic figure, from beaten, groveling Jew to man of Hebrew dignity. Few characters in Shakespeare's plays lend themselves to such a vast range of interpretation.

For a long while the role was always played with a red wig, a tradition dating back, presumably, to the premiering of the part by Burbage in Shakespeare's time.

The red-wig tradition was broken dramatically by Edwin Kean in 1814, who not only played Shylock in a black wig for the first time, but played him with such fire and savagery as to electrify all London. It is said that Kean was an impecunious player at the time, and the black-wig innovation may have been owing purely to the fact that he had a black wig and could not afford the price of a red one. Obviously the wig was incidental to his tradition-shattering interpretation of the role.

If Shakespeare could have been looking across a couple of centuries, he probably would have cheered Kean for smashing another Shylock tradition, which apparently got started in the early eighteenth century when an actor named Dogget played the role as a comic figure. There seems little evidence that Shakespeare ever intended Shylock to be the Falstaff or Nick Bottom of the play. Humor he has, but not buffoonery. Yet the Dogget tradition doggedly persisted until an actor named Macklin restored the Venetian Jew to a forceful reality, preparing an interpretation that was so daring that he saved it to spring on his cast on

Gratiano and Lorenzo, *The Merchant of Venice*

opening night. One wonders who was the more astounded —his audience or his fellow actors. Today such thunderstriking audacity would hardly win favor in professional circles.

Sir Henry Irving's Shylock is worth noting because it was, by all accounts, at once theatrically effective yet foreign to the textual implication. He played the Jew for all the pathos he could squeeze into the part, rounding things out with a tear-jerking exit from the trial scene—a broken, downtrodden, beaten moneylender. Such treatment of the famous role may heighten the melodrama and bring handkerchiefs to eyes, but somehow we don't believe that that is quite what Shakespeare had in mind.

Sir Henry probably let the "Hath not a Jew eyes? . . . If you prick us do we not bleed? . . . if you poison us do we not die? And if you wrong us, shall we not revenge?" speech carry him to a distorted concept of the character. All of which is a reminder that even the finest actors are sometimes misled by lines and lose sight of the overall impact of the play.

Yet who would be so reckless as to lay down rules for Shylock? The only governor an actor has is Shakespeare himself, and the actor's own good taste and aesthetic judgment. Shylock has been played a thousand ways, and there are, no doubt, yet a thousand more interpretations to be discovered.

New eyes will see him in new light, new minds will find what others may have missed. The last great Shylock has not come and gone, nor has the world seen the ultimate Portia. So long as there are young players stretching toward greatness, there will arise, from time to time, great performances of these and all of Shakespeare's characters. The impetus is in the bard's creations.

Directors, like their actor-manager counterparts before them, have a proclivity to postulate. They are sometimes inclined to take a political or social stance, and seek to shape a play to fit that stance. The current pressure to make everything relevant encourages such tendencies. To shape a play to say something that is meaningful now is a temptation that does not always go away when told "get thee behind me." Productions pertinent to the times have popular appeal, and plays, after all, are dependent upon playgoers. Shakespeare, being susceptible to diverse postulations, is often victim. Oh, the hanky panky, the weird distortions, the plagues of plagiarism that go on in the name of William Shakespeare!

The Merchant of Venice is one of his plays that lend themselves particularly to postulations. But there is good news for postulators. They need not strain and stretch and make a shamble of the text of this or any of the bard's great plays. The great, the exciting thing about Shakespeare is his relevance to life, life in his time, life in our time, life in any time.

If we will but let his people speak, and hew to the truth inherent in his texts, we need no foisting of fake imposition. The relevance is there, and needs no superimposition. Shakespeare is meaningful—NOW.

The truth is, faithfulness to Shakespeare is, in itself, quite task enough for anyone to tackle.

The Merchant of Venice

DIRECTING CONCEPT

This controversial comedy has been sometimes considered anti-Jewish and sometimes anti-Christian. Surely a man with Shakespeare's apparent compassion could not have been anti-anybody. He was too big for bigotry. It seems obvious enough that he meant *The Merchant of*

Venice to be exactly what it is—a play with conflict, multi-dimensional characters, comedy, romance, and overtones of tragedy and satire. Ergo, we present it thus.

This is theatre, towering through time, dynamic, romantic, dramatic theatre reaching out to heart and mind. This is Shakespeare speaking from the timeless stage, speaking contemporaneously, as he always does, telling a tale of far away and long ago.

Once upon a time there was a place where lust of life led men to do both savage and unselfish acts, and lovely ladies graced their acts with grandeur and enchantment. The place was Venice, Italy, not the sinking Venice of the latter days, but the bold, resplendent Venice of the Renaissance. Revival of the Greco-Roman classics clashed with

Salarino, Shylock, and Tubal, *The Merchant of Venice*

the Christian concepts of medieval times, and people, calling themselves Christian, swaggered their way toward the new freedom of enlightenment, that lighted their way to affluence and self-centered self-realization. A man might lay down his life for a friend, but friend joined friend to crush an enemy.

The camaraderie among the new nobility was rich with sweet Franciscan love, but love among the virile young burst into passion when the goal was a golden fleece. New Testament lessons learned, though charily remembered, rose to the rescue with self-righteous zest when an eye for an eye, or a tooth for a tooth, or a bond for a pound of flesh was at stake. It was a time and place for bold and blatant proclamation, for proclamation of one's faith or love or hate, and for rich, poetic ornamentation of one's proclamation. One ornamented speech as one ornamented dress and manners, or homes and gardens, and even gondolas.

Along the rich Rialto, along the gaily poled canals, life was colorful, lush, and lusty, and it was a place and time for high adventure and grandiose romance.

Antonio, a wealthy playboy merchant, weary with feasts and nightly frolics, might readily risk a few thousand ducats to launch a youthful friend in matrimony, especially when the matrimonial prize was a lady wooed by every prince in Europe. Why should a ransom as ridiculous as a pound of his fair flesh prevent him? A Jewish jest was just a plum to him, and he would have the laugh on Shylock when his ships came home, and fun at that curmudgeonous usurer's expense would be fun indeed.

To Bassanio the jest has a sinister sound, but he is enamored and dead broke, so is easily assured that all will be well.

Before night falls the Venetian streets will ring with

the rumor of the deal and it will be a whopping good tale well calculated for a laugh among the Jewish moneylenders. Old Shylock has outfoxed that thorn in the Jewish flesh, Antonio. A pound of Christian flesh—what comical collateral! The mood of merriment and colorful romance is set, and it is against that mood that the tragic interlude intrudes.

The witty, pretty belle of Belmont, richly left, is wooed and won, but beyond the sun-filled afternoons and starlit nights the threatening clouds collect. The storm will break, imperiling ships at sea, but, before the wind, a storm of a more personal nature will strike the home of the lonely widower, Shylock. His daughter, Jessica—loved dearly, like all his dear possessions, and all-too-greedily protected and possessèd, too strictly sheltered from the Christians—is a joyful Jewess, too spirited, too bewitching, and far too much dominated by her sire not to give eye and ear and even heart to Lorenzo, a likely lad who likely says "Have gondola, will travel."

They travel light, Lorenzo and his infidel, as light as ducats, gems, and jewelry allow, and thus seduction springs the storm that soon engulfs the romance and the romanticists with intrigue and involvement. The dashing, joy-loving, aristocratic cohorts of Antonio win their loves and win the wrath of Shylock, and in their winning, lose for their beloved Antonio all hope of charity or clemency from Shylock.

The storm is on and the storm center is the hardened heart of a lonely, selfish, hard-bitten Jew, betrayed, bedeviled, embarrassed, and disgraced. Armed to the teeth with knife and scales and justice in his gaberdine, he means to play for keeps, taking this opportunity to rid himself and Venice of the merchant who is a hindrance to his busi-

Casket scene, *The Merchant of Venice.*
COURTESY PARMENTER STUDIOS

ness, and at the same time, wreaking vengeance on the Christians from whom he has learned vengeance.

To travel to the court disguised as judge and clerk, and see their husbands before they see them, may have been a Portian prank when first conceived, but in the sobering, sinister surroundings of the trial, a woman with the wit and wisdom and the loving heart of Portia draws on her depth of character to rise to heights she never dreamed were there. Almost before she knows what's happening, she is in beyond her depth, and in sheer desperation seeks frantically for some loop-hole in the law, some jot of jurisprudence that will save the life of her husband's dearest friend and render justice. Only when the knife is at Antonio's heart does Portia find the legal passage barely in time to cry in thrilling triumph "Tarry a little!", and in the split second of that cry, reverse the course of events.

The Jew will have all justice, but justice now, thanks to Portia's brilliance and persistence, begins to favor the merchant, favoring him so fully that in the end the very life of Shylock hangs on a word of mercy from the Duke, so he is allowed to quit the court, disgraced and dispossessed but not quite finally and utterly defeated. No melodramatic antagonist shuffling off in sentimental penitence, no tear-jerking exit for a man of his dimension. Bloody but unbowed, he will get another toe-hold somewhere, sometime. But now Portia, Antonio, the Duke, and the Court are rid of him, and the focus returns to the victors, and the fun begins again.

The storm has passed, devastating and violent as it was —or threatened to be; the storm has passed and the moon shines bright across the enchanted Belmont gardens, and Hyman, god of love, rules o'er the revels.

The story told, we see that he for whom the play is titled is pivotal to the plot, but the play is blend of comedy, romance, and threat of tragedy, and spiriting all elements toward climax and conclusion is Portia, gracious, noble, fun-loving, touching the lives of all who chance within her orbit, like the grey-eyed goddess guiding Odysseus. Yet, unlike Athena, Portia grows, going from carefree flirtations to character fulfillment of love and mature responsibility, abetted all the way by the sparkle and the charm of her maid and companion, Nerissa. She will be queen bee to Bassanio, though never sting so much as steer and even serve, and he will be both lord and slave to her, enslaved by his enamored heart, yet striding like the lord he is, a man more suitably substantial than most adventurers and fortune hunters.

Bassanio, Antonio, and Shylock, *The Merchant of Venice*

His friends, Gratiano, Lorenzo, Salanio, Salarino, and Salerio are loyal, lusty, life-loving youths of noble blood much on the town, ever ready for a rumble, and always in pursuit of pleasure and excitement, yet with character enough to have concern for one another and for their mentor, the merchant.

The "Sal boys," the Mods of ancient Venice, insensitive to the suffering of Shylock and all too ready to taunt and mock him, are sensitive enough to Antonio's plight, one rushing to his side, another hurrying to Belmont to bear the merchant's letter to Bassanio.

Lorenzo, protesting that Gratiano never lets him speak, speaks well enough to win the mischievous Jessica, and articulates his love in language as beautiful as the moon-filled night that envelops his love-making. Self-centered poet lover that he is, he never seems to realize that his elopement with Jessica adds peril to Antonio's plight. A pair of thoughtless, inconsiderate scamps, he and his Jessica are so in love that we are caught up in their idyllic amour and accept, if not excuse, them.

Acceptable also is the nonconscientious conduct of Launcelot who, budged more by fiend than conscience, abets the Jessica-Lorenzo rendezvous and leaves the service of old Shylock for the service of young Bassanio, a nifty, shifty deal in sheer chicanery. Clowning his way through life, Gratiano is the first to try to cheer Antonio into a brighter mood, and first to rail against the Jew in court. Generous in spirit as he is with words and wit, he wants to go with Bassanio to Belmont, promising to curb his impulsive tendency to ever play the fool, but it may be that he has been in Belmont once before and has remembrance of a pretty girl he saw there in the house of Portia. Bright, cocky extrovert that he is, he tells us as the story starts, and tells us in the end, too, that all the action, somber though it is at times, is framed in comedy and romance.

How can he and all the others in that final scene indulge in such frivolity after the tense drama of the trial? Well, they have been through purgatory with old Shylock and are a little giddy with relief to find themselves in something of a heaven with all things working out delightfully.

Queen of the revels is, of course, the handsome, gracious

To Tell Again of Shylock and Fair Portia

heiress whom many Jasons wooed in vain. There was the serious, smoldering, and sonorous Moroccan prince, "too grieved," he says, but probably too proud, "to take a proper leave"; and the arrogant, foppish prince of Aragon, cocksure until he draws the portrait of a blinking idiot from the casket and leaves in humorous castigation of himself.

It is a tribute to the young lord who runs her estate that Portia calls herself Balthasar as judge, and an indication, no doubt, of her esteem for him. He is obviously more than a major-domo and he takes his responsibilities earnestly and with enthusiasm. In a sense, Balthasar is to Portia what Tubal is to Shylock, a handy thing to have

Jessica and Lorenzo, *The Merchant of Venice.*
COURTESY PARMENTER STUDIOS

around, though Portia probably has more affection for him than Shylock has for Tubal.

It is Tubal who saves the play from being an anti-Jewish play. He is Jewish to the hilt, with his sly but cutting humor, his cunning, and his readiness to lend money to a fellow Hebrew, but he heightens the aloneness of Shylock by not bothering to turn up at the trial, and accents the fact that Shylock, Jew or no Jew, is a selfish old scoundrel by taunting him with news that is alternately good and bad. In that brief conversation he is saying to Shylock virtually, "You are a fellow moneylender and a member of my race, so I will lend you money and go in search of your runaway daughter; but you are an old skinflint and you are getting just what you have coming to you."

Once upon a time in the make-believe of theatre, a powerful, poetic, amusing, and romantic tale was told, an oft-told tale now trimmed with great tradition. So let us tell it once again, tell it on the old Rialto, in the domicile of Portia, the courtyard of the Duke, and in the enchanted Belmont garden. Let us tell the tale with color and with light, and with the sound of song and tinkling mandolins. In the magic mood of moonlight, the light of sunlit afternoons and starlight, in movement majestic and amusing, and in language lyrical and immortal, let us tell again the story of fair Portia and old Shylock.

3
Of Lovers, Artisans, and Sprites

For several seasons we opened the summer series at the beautiful Redlands Bowl with *A Midsummer Night's Dream,* replete with large cast, symphony orchestra, chorus, and corps de ballet. The natural amphitheatre setting, with colonnades flanking the open Grecian stage was, one might readily suppose, something that Shakespeare might have approved. There among the shrubs and carved stone benches the action of the play moved easily from the palace of the Duke into the fairy woodlands and back again.

As on the stages of the Elizabethans, the language of the play furnished all necessary scenery. Night cloaking the surrounding park was her own enchantress, and "the moon, new bent in Heaven," was moon enough to help Puck cast his magic spells.

There were no lords and ladies flanking the wings as on the stage of Shakespeare's time, but there were children edging up the grassy banks to better their enthrallment. Those Bowl productions were family affairs, and parents, filling the regular seats, were glad to be rid for a while of their wiggling youngsters. Sometimes the children cluttered the entrance of the fairies, but fairies and children have always shared the selfsame world, and Oberon and Titania were delighted.

Year after year, the play that once charmed Queen Elizabeth the First charmed citizens and guests from near and far, even as it has charmed millions of playgoers in thousands of places through hundreds of years.

Not all productions of *A Midsummer Night's Dream* have been so simply staged. Indeed, some of our own have called for much more elaborate sets, but excessive realistic scenery is always a hazard to this play. Its delicately ethereal quality is fragile. The flower-like fragility of Titania can be easily crushed. Peaseblossom, Cobweb, and Mustard Seed are pure thistledown, and want the touch of wand and not the hammer blows of stage carpenters.

Puck needs no clumsy fog machine to lead the lovers "up and down, up and down. Robin lead them up and down," and Oberon needs no actual bank where the wild thyme grows, not with such poetry as Shakespeare has given him to tell about it. This is a fairy tale and should be told as such, and the telling of a fairy tale calls only for imagination.

Such scenery as will create a mood is fine, a mood that suggests, but does not specify. To spell a forest out in hard stones and trees and brush, to make a palace with three dimensional pillars, is to lay heavy hand on the enchantment of illusion. We dare not lose illusion lest we lose the dream.

Although we have not always been so (the concept below being indicative of an exception), we were conventional in our Bowl productions of *A Midsummer Night's Dream*. A full production with the Felix Mendelssohn music and

Final scene, *A Midsummer Night's Dream.*
COURTESY DAVID UMBACH

fairy dances seemed right for that particular audience and setting. Even the Mendelssohn Wedding March, sung by a chorus composed of ladies and gentlemen of Duke Theseus's court, rounded out the last scene in a grand finale. It all made for a colorful spectacle and magnificent sound, and it could be argued that if Shakespeare had had the Mendelssohn score and a symphony orchestra with chorus at his disposal, he would in all probability have used them. In his time symphonies were still a century or so away, and his instruments were limited to recorders, mandolins, viola da gambas, lutes and flutes and drums and horns, and a few viols and zithers. Songs were simple and melodious. Nevertheless, he made ingenious use of the music of his period.

Use of such period music in productions today seems wearisome to some, but it does give a production historic authenticity.

Titania and Bottom, *A Midsummer Night's Dream.*
COURTESY DAVID UMBACH

One final reference to our Bowl productions of *A Midsummer Night's Dream* may be of special interest to our readers. The reference is to one of our Titanias—a highly talented girl and quite right for the part, except that we sometimes felt that she should have been playing Puck because of her mischievousness and her inclination to shinny up the lighting poles between her entrances. Time after time in rehearsals, she would be late for her cue because she would be atop a pole. No, she was no tomboy. On the contrary she was as feminine as anyone could wish a fairy queen to be, but at thirteen she liked to climb and play pranks.

She tried our patience, but she was good in the role and we were particularly impressed with her singing voice, and padded her part a bit to give our audiences the benefit of that remarkable talent. The audiences loved her, though little did they know, and little did we know, that the Titania of that summer would, in a few years, become the famous Joan Baez, folk singer preeminent, and nationally known crusader for peace.

A Midsummer Night's Dream

DIRECTING CONCEPT

More masque than play, the *Dream* is what the name implies, a dream, a charming, colorful, comical dream of sheer enchantment. It is love-smitten youth romping romantically through moon-drenched woodlands. It is love at its zenith as Theseus and Hippolyta celebrate their nuptials, love in mischievous madness in the Fairy Kingdom, and it is clowning at its most comical in the hands of "hard-handed men who never labored in their minds till now."

It is "all in jollity," this jestful idyl of nonsense and romance. It wants, always and forever, the light touch, the lilt of laughter even in the tears of despair, the wand of magic that weaves a spell, and the forthright humor that rocks the ground with jocund sound. Poetic it is, with unequaled imagery. Romantic it is, radiant with the sparkling phosphorescence of fantasy. But heavy? Never!

Even the threat of death or celibacy confronting Hermia, or the horrendous frustration engulfing Helena, or the furious altercation dividing Titania and Oberon, must have the lyrical lift, the gleeful glide in voice and movement. It is pretend. It is all delirious, delectable, delightful "let's pretend." It is magical, mischievous make-believe in the land of Never-Never.

Where is this Never-Never land? In ancient Greece? In Athens? In the sylvan haunts of Pan, long, long ago? Perhaps, but only perhaps. The where and when are only just that—"perhaps." The where is there in the nether world of dream. The when is now or any time when souls take time to soar through the realms of the risible, the fanciful, the romantic. Therefore, the palace of Duke Theseus is a patch of color somewhere in a sunlit afternoon, a place where fluted pillars shimmer and become translucent shapes of trees, and objects seen for what they are in daylight are not what they are at all when "the moon looks with a watery eye." Sounds that pass for song and laughter in the court of Theseus become the nymph-like music of night-time woods when Puck and Oberon are at their mischief.

Of Lovers, Artisans, and Sprites

Titania, Bottom, and Fairies, *A Midsummer Night's Dream.*
COURTESY DAVID UMBACH

Moving through gossamer and lacy leaves, the gracefully garmented lovers dance—their costumes, in modified Renaissance style, falling in folds or following the flow of movement, movement that is clearly choreographed.

The three converging conflicts, involving love in pursuit of love, pride against pride, and hams plotting a play, compile the simple though entangling story line.

Hermia wants Lysander and Helena wants Demetrius. Oberon demands a little changeling child, which Titania will not give up to him. Quince and his fellows are bent on performing for the Duke, with that ham of hams, Nick Bottom, wanting to play all the roles himself.

Puck, resembling Cupid, Pan, and Peck's Bad Boy, consorts in devilment with Oberon, playing a prank or two on his own.

But out of it all "Jack shall have Jill, naught shall go ill, the man shall have his mare again, and all will be well."

4
When Witches Work Their Evil Spell

Today any one who blames witches for his bad behavior is likely to be hustled off to a psychiatric ward. The spell of black magic is no longer excuse enough for doing evil deeds. This side of Freud, we have to face the fact that the fault lies in ourselves, not in our stars or in some evil witchcraft. Even a wrong deed done on a drug trip is usually indefensible in court.

We take this modern viewpoint so for granted that it is difficult to realize that only a short while ago it was common practice to assume that persons could be possessed of demons.

Years after Shakespeare, centuries in fact, people, even reasonable people, still believed in witchcraft. We have our witch hunts, to be sure, but they are usually intended to punish some nonconforming critic of the system. Once witch hunts were for witches, and witches, it was thought, might be anywhere, but most especially in lonely moors on misty nights, or when the wind howled and the distant thunder rumbled.

On such a night three weird old women might send shivers down the spine were one to encounter them, even

Lady Macbeth and Macbeth, *Macbeth*

now, alone. But in the misty past when the Thane of Glamis (Macbeth) walked with a friend on "so foul and fair a day," the shivers were almost like the shakes.

Let us accept at once the fact that witches, to Elizabethan audiences, were as acceptable as kings. The common people believed in witches as they believed in God. No doubt there were a few among the intellectuals of the time who were disbelievers, but if they voiced their skepticism about witches, they were suspected of subversion. Accept the acceptability of witches and your appreciation of *Macbeth* will be enhanced.

In what is presumed to be the last of Shakespeare's tragedies, the power of darkness prevails. The supernatural forces drench the play in darkness and in blood. The very air is poisoned with fears and growing hatred. Thoughts black lead to deeds terrible as guests are murdered, feasting turns to horror, and innocent sleep turns into nightmare. We need no incantation to carry us with the villains to their inevitable destruction. The lady of the Thane takes care of that.

"Come, you spirits that tend on mortal thoughts, unsex me here, and fill me from the crown to the toe top-full of direst cruelty. . . . Come to my woman's breast and take my milk for gall, you murdering ministers, wherever in your sightless substances you wait on nature's mischief! Come, thick night, and pall thee in the dunnest smoke of hell, that my keen knife see not the wound it makes, nor Heaven peep through the blanket of the dark to cry, 'Hold, hold.'"

Marlowe's Dr. Faustus invoked the devil. Lady Macbeth's invocation seems to have been to hell itself, and hell responded, releasing all its sightless substances promptly and with a vengeance. They soon possess the lady and use her precisely as she imprecated. They come, these demons, making of her the relentless creature she has herself envisioned. They come, veiling the stars and filling the blackened night with terror. She will goad her lord to do the deed, to screw his courage to the sticking point, and do the bloody deed.

The hags of hell have worked their spell, holding in their evil clutches the miserable Macbeth.

Of course we no longer believe in witches, and hell itself is somewhat out of style with many, but for the brief span of this, his shortest tragedy, Shakespeare comes close to making us converts to black magic. That he does is to his credit and to our enjoyment, if enjoyment is the word for describing one's reaction to this spellbinding play.

It is thought that Shakespeare lifted his witches straight out of a witchcraft book of his time, a book no doubt familiar to many, if not most, of his playgoers. Even King James the First, who by the time of *Macbeth* had come down from Scotland to occupy the throne made vacant by Elizabeth's death, even King James wrote a treatise about witchcraft. Even the king was gullible to old wives' tales, and no doubt believed the rumor that two hundred witches set out with a sieve to sink the ship bearing his queen from Denmark.

This tragedy, tight as a Bach fugue, and as concise as *King Lear* is sprawling, is a murder thriller without peer, and it is no wonder that its impact has had the strange effect on actors it is said to have had. There is a long tradition among old troupers to the effect that no one in the theatre should ever quote from *Macbeth*. To quote a line from that play backstage, in green room, or in dressing quarters is a certain sign of bad luck. It's worse than whistling, another longtime backstage taboo.

Young actors nowadays do not go along with such super-

When Witches Work Their Evil Spell 67

stitions, of course, but many a tyro has shivered nonetheless to hear some old stage veteran tell of the terrible things that have happened to players and productions where such lines as "lay on, Macduff" and "when shall we three meet again" have been carelessly uttered.

Banquo and Macbeth, *Macbeth*

Was it a careless slip that caused our slight disaster? In one of our productions of *Macbeth* we had a blooper that was as funny as it was embarrassing. In Act IV, Scene I the witches treat Macbeth to a spectacle of apparitions forecasting his ominous future. One in particular sounds a warning that leads to the mass murder of Lady Macduff and her innocent children, hence the line the apparition speaks is a key line.

The actress then playing the role has subsequently gone on to do outstanding work, but she was at the time young and very nervous. The line that is the motivation for Macbeth's immediate action is "Macbeth, Macbeth, beware Macduff!" Simple. Anyone with a voice could be expected to get that out. How could she miss? Well, she did. On opening night the line came out, "Macbeth, Macbeth, beware Macbeth!" Not quite the same!

Embarrassed to tears, and determined to get it right the second night, she "screwed her courage to the sticking point" and proclaimed loud and clear, "Macduff, Macduff, beware . . . ," then, aware of her dreadful boo-boo, ended the line so that it came out "Macduff, Macduff, beware Mac!"

"Mac" we called her for the rest of the run. Thereafter, it must be added, "Macbeth, Macbeth, beware Macduff" came out all right, but that was one line from the play that defied the ancient superstition. Everyone in the cast was saying it, by way of pre-prompting the unhappy actress.

The action of *Macbeth* is Grecian in its forthright prescience of impending doom. The narrative, like a great wind, sweeps everyone toward a foreseeable abyss. Weird women hail Macbeth, who is Thane of Glamis, as Thane of Cawdor, and predict he will be king. Macbeth is then made Thane of Cawdor by Duncan, King of Scots. Prompted by Lady Macbeth, Macbeth kills Duncan, casting suspicion on Duncan's sons, who flee, and is himself crowned.

Fearing the prediction that heirs of Banquo shall be kings, Macbeth has Banquo murdered, but his ghost haunts the banquet table at the coronation feast, and Macbeth resolves to seek out the witches for further counsel.

The mischief-making witches tell Macbeth that none of

When Witches Work Their Evil Spell

Hecuba and the Witches, *Macbeth*

woman born shall harm Macbeth and that he shall reign till Birnam Wood is removed to Dunsinane. But he is warned to beware Macduff. Learning that Macduff has fled to England, but fearful of his heirs, the power-mad Macbeth has Lady Macduff and her children put to death. Learning of this in England, where he and Malcolm, Duncan's heir apparent, are raising an army to combat the tyrant Macbeth, Macduff resolves, with Malcolm, to return and overpower Macbeth.

Overcome with guilt, Lady Macbeth walks and talks in her sleep, revealing incriminating information anent the evil she and her king have done together.

Macduff and Malcolm, backed by the English force,

return, and Siward, the British general, orders every soldier to cut branches from the Birnam Wood and advance on Dunsinane. Hearing that the woods are moving toward him, Macbeth is terrified. Then comes the news that his queen is dead.

Desperate, but still convinced that no man born of woman can harm him, Macbeth encounters Macduff, who announces that he was "from his mother's womb untimely ripp'd." They fight, Macbeth is slain, and Malcolm, Duncan's rightful heir, is hailed King of Scotland.

The Tragedy of Macbeth

DIRECTING CONCEPT

It is night on the fogbound island of medieval Scotland, night in the minds of men in the mist of superstition.

Deep in the mind of every man lies a fertile seed of self-destruction, a death wish grappling with the will to live. Deep in the primitive will to survive surges the urge to conquest, the urge toward unrestrained dominion.

Had there been no Thane and wife with evil dreams the good king Duncan might have continued to reign, his grace dispelling gloom. But dark deeds cloud the purity of light in ancient Scotland.

The murderous Scottish thane lived long ago, yet lives again each time his tragedy is told, and in the living bestirs the Thane of Cawdor that lurks within the slumbering consciousness of every man.

A man, a Scottish statesman, innocent enough at first, doing his job like any ordinary man, proving extraordinary in battle, is, with a fellow lord, on his way to Forres. The weather is both foul and fair. The two suddenly come upon three weird sisters. In the dusk of dismal afternoon they are readily recognized as witches.

Then, with the conjuring, comes the questioning: ill or good? Who counts prognostication ill when it brings earnest of success? Besides, with half the forecast soon confirmed by Ross, why should not the newly pronounced Thane of Cawdor believe the other half: "Thou shalt be King?"

"The charm's wound up," and a valiant, noble man is now entangled, and he will go from evil deed to deeds more evil in his nightmare entanglement that impels toward destruction.

At last the night is over, the long, evil, starless night. A clean, fresh wind dispels the "fog and filthy air" and Scots can breathe in hope again.

We tell our savage story simply, strongly, starkly, playing out the action in sound and light and shadow. We tell it on slabs of Highland stone that can be crags or castle steps, dark caverns or dunes of Dunsinane.

We tell, and in the telling, tell how yesterdays "have lighted fools the way to dusty death," the fools who rule by brutal force.

5
Spirits Who Lift the Soul to Light

In *The Tempest,* we soar to sunlit heights. Yet, as in *Macbeth,* we are aided by the supernatural. This time, however, in the hands of banished Duke Prospero the magic works good. Here is enchantment in all the rainbow colors. Here the mist is sun-drenched, and the mystery is in a mode of pure delight.

The Tempest, more than the others perhaps, is a play for readers. In this play readers may give their minds a limitless feast of fancy. Imaginations are free to conjure all that Prospero, with wand and book, can conjure, and as much more as their fantasies may afford. The storm, a palatable prologue, may roar as loudly or as gently as the reader chooses, and all the ensuing adventure can make the sounds and sights of the island pathways to adventures never ending. The lyricism of *The Tempest* sings itself into the very souls of all who read the singing words.

Yet, those words were written to be spoken, and on the tongues of actors attuned to such lyricism, the words make most unearthly music.

". . . the isle is full of noises, sounds, and sweet airs, that give delight and hurt not. Sometimes a thousand twangling instruments will hum about mine ears," as Caliban says, "and sometimes voices, that, if I then had waked after long sleep, will make me sleep again; and then, in dreaming, the clouds, methought, would open and show riches ready to drop upon me: that, when I waked, I cried to dream again."

So do we, watching or reading the play, cry to dream again when the last line of the play ends our dream. They are, indeed—those people of this enchanting play—"such stuff as dreams are made on," suggesting that we who view and we who read may also be but the substance of a dream, figments of fiction in the vague remembrance of some god. This play gets to us in ways like that, for in that strange sea-scented island there are byways between the ways the players take, and caverns beyond the cave of Caliban. No wonder that, between the lines, we wander with our minds.

There has been no end to the speculation on the symbolism of *The Tempest*. There are the obvious observations linking Caliban with earth, Ariel with air, and Prospero with the age-old mystery of water; or letting Prospero stand for intellect, Ariel for spirit, and Caliban for flesh. The play is a veritable field trip for symbol hunters, and on that island of pure fancy, the hunting is good. The elements of water, earth, and air are there ready for poetic investigation.

There is the sea, the hint of mist and rain, the probability of cool, clear springs, there are the rocks, the moss, the trees, and growing things, the trusty terra firma, and there is the clean, flower-scented air, sun warmed and wind cooled, much like the air of Capri, some think, while others think of Maui or some Pacific island farther south. Of course, Shakespeare never heard of Maui, and it isn't likely he ever visited Capri, but somehow the essence of those islands came to him. But the basic elements of life are central to the play, making the play all the more central to all-breathing life.

World navigators brought tales from far-off places to London streets and inns, and Shakespeare was a man with ears. The sight and sound and feel and smell of other worlds were his to tap, as were great sources for his plots. The story of a banished duke of Milan may have come to him ready made, or it may have been a patched-up piece of many tales. Whatever may have been its source, *The Tempest* is one of his rarest gems, a gem to crown the literature of the world.

Settings for *The Tempest* can be anything, or everything, or nothing but a bare space on a floor or patch of ground. However, the last time we produced the play it was a designing thesis for one of our majors. What designer wouldn't go to town with such a play? Ours did. Because he did, we had a problem. In that problem is a story worth repeating—the story of Ariel.

In deference to the designer's thesis, we conceived the production with a flying Ariel. Accordingly, the flying gear was purchased and installed, the system tested, the flymen trained, and numerous test runs were made with the heaviest bodies we could find making the tests. There was no problem with the gear or with the flying team. The gear worked perfectly, the men were quick to acquire the necessary carefulness and precision. All systems were "Go," except for our flying Ariel.

She couldn't fly! She had her role down pat, was perfect in the part, but the poor girl was terrified at the thought of being whisked from off-stage to on, from towering hill-top to floor and up again and off, all at breathtaking speed. She tried. She must be credited for bravely trying, but each trial flight made her panic and freeze up. We did not know, and she did not know when she was cast that she actually had flight-phobia.

Discovery of the frightening fact came much too late. Such crises always come too late. We had less than a week before the opening when we finally faced reality. Too late? Nothing in the theatre can ever be too late. Impossibility is a word not often heard in back-stage circles.

The awful moment of truth came late one afternoon when the 210-pound man who served as counterweight barely escaped serious injury. It was essential that Ariel streak through the air like a jet in flight. To accomplish this the counterweight man simply stepped off his off-stage tower just under the grid, and, holding the lead-line, dropped to the floor where an air mattress broke his fall—broke it, that is, when Ariel was on the other end.

On cue he leaped, but Ariel did not. She never left her spot. Somehow, in her panic, she had failed to snap the fly line to her harness, so our 210-pounder hit the floor with a thud that jarred the entire stage. His fall was a good twenty feet. In spite of that he was not hurt, other than the ache he felt in every muscle the next day.

One of the problems in directing is knowing when to act, and then acting. Do we scrap the whole idea of an air-borne Ariel? Too late for that. It would have meant reblocking throughout the show. Do we try to help our Ariel to overcome her fear? That might be dangerous, since we are not psychologists. Do we take her out of the role at the last minute, and cause her great unhappiness? We know she loves the role. We know she wants to fly, but by now we know she can't. She knows it too, and faces the bitter truth with us in a teary, troubling session. Once out of the play, of course, she felt relief that compensated for her disappointment.

So there we were without an Ariel, with a sold-out opening looming ominously. No, our Ariel had no understudy. There were flyers, plenty of them. Nearly every girl in the theatre had volunteered for test flights from time to time.

One in particular had taken to it so beautifully, it was hard to keep her out of the harness. We look her over. We know her, know her acting, but we look her over and over and over again. Her size is right, she is petite and very pretty. But can she do an Ariel? More to the point, can she do an Ariel in so short a time?

We hear her read. She sounds read-y, but has a lovely and well-projected voice. She reads again. She takes direction, takes it well. She wants the part. That's clear. She wants the part so badly she could cry. Don't cry. Just read, and read again. You're sounding better, dear. Still, steady. We must not cast out of desperation. Desperation! We laugh at that. Desperation is what we've got aplenty. Still, can she do it? Can this little darling turn herself into an Ariel in a few short rehearsals, or even a few long rehearsals? She tells us that she can. She tells us with her voice and with her eyes and with her graceful, flyable body. She's in! The show is on! Ariel will fly tonight.

So our plucky little dancing lady saves the show and joins the long, long list of Ariels remembered and forgotten.

The Tempest

DIRECTING CONCEPT

Mind and magic may maneuver, but only compassion begets reconciliation. Reconciliation is the object of the maneuvering, but there is more to the reconciliation than the return of a banished duke to his rightful dukedom. There is a marriageable princess to account for, a princess who has grown to maturity on a deserted island sans contact with all human beings save her father and a deformed monster who fain would have peopled the isle with sons by her, except for the wisdom of her father.

Idyllic as life is on the isle of Prospero's enchantment, he, Prospero, must find a new life for his child, Miranda, a life to be shared with a husband, and a husband worthy of her stature and station.

It is the maidenhood of Miranda, and a hoped-for flowering of that maidenhood, and a future for the lovely young daughter in a "brave new world," that provoke the mischief of the tempest. Out of that mischief comes the shipwreck, comes Prince Ferdinand to woo the maiden, comes the confrontation of villains and heroes, comes the comic trickery of clowns and Caliban, and comes, eventually the drowning of the book of magic and the freeing of the celestial Ariel.

The storm, therefore, is primal. It is the vortex from which action springs. Combers, wind, and thunder crash all around us as darkness descends, a darkness broken only by whips of lightning and a single, constant, mystic light on the banished Duke and daughter as they survey the tempest from their towering vantage, a vantage from which the wizard, Prospero, literally commands and conducts the storm while the terrified Miranda looks on in fascination.

The storm over, the ship split and abandoned, the darkness lifts, and we behold the island, a mass of wooded crags and rocks sunlit through a frame of giant foliage. There, in the hollow of a cliff, is Prospero's cell, appearing and vanishing with the shifting light. There too is the tree trunk that becomes Caliban, and there the gossamer mist and drifting iridescent dust through which the dancing Ariel flies.

The storm, though over, is still at Prospero's command as residual rumblings frequently are heard and shadowy storm clouds still enchant the isle with shifting light that turns one patch of island into another as the now thundering, now singing surf blends with the strange bird calls, the weird, ethereal music, and the many other island sounds.

Under the spell of sun and shade and sea and sounds, the stranded voyagers breathe the fragrant tropical air and are intoxicated, more by air than drink, and those who drink are giddy more from rapture than from wine. Even their rapture is more mischievous than malicious, although the sluggish, enslaved Caliban is ready enough to surrender to a new master, and there is malice, assuredly, in the minds of Antonio and Sebastian as they draw their swords against the slumbering king, Alonzo, and the kind old Gonzalo.

On such an isle, conjured by such a one as Prospero, there must be nymphs and sprites and even goddesses, and they, like Ariel, appear and vanish at the will of the master necromancer, both to astound and to enthrall. They, like the drifting mist, strange music, and unearthly sounds, are as indigenous as Caliban, and, like the "fishy" fellow, are subject ever to the mind and wand of Prospero.

For Prospero, the mind and wand are one. He has not come lately to his wizardry. Indeed, it was his bookishness that lost him his dukedom, and, when his reign is again restored to him, he will, no doubt, find new intellectual pursuits, even though he will turn his back on conjuring. He is more scholar than prince, but he is more father than scholar. So he will use his wizardry to win a better life for his child, and, for her sake, resume the responsibility of rule. Rivaling his filial love is his fondness for Ariel, who is the embodiment of all his scholarly achievements on the island. Yet he has promised Ariel that she would one day be free, and in spite of the amity the blithe spirit feels for the master, freedom is an ever-growing longing.

No one need wonder at the love encounter of Prince Ferdinand and Miranda. He is the first young man her virgin eyes have ever seen. In the radiance of her beholding she would be beautiful enough even without the island spell that brings the Prince to where she is. It is indubitably love at first sight, and a love the Prince is pleased to prove under Papa Prospero's testing indenture. No complications cloud their hearts with doubt. Their love is poetry, pure and serene.

Far from serene is the love of Alonzo for his son. His

love for Ferdinand is drenched with inner tears of despair as he concludes that his heir is lost at sea. He cannot know the lonely longing his son is feeling for his father, whom he believes also lost at sea. Nor can the loyalty of faithful Gonzalo comfort the King as they wander the isle unaware of the threat to life their treacherous companions pose.

Treachery makes blood brothers of Sebastian and Antonio, a treachery fanned both by the goading of the latter and by the ambition of the former. They are usurpers, pure and simple, though certainly less pure than simple. The darkness of their villainy adumbrates the grace of Prospero's forgiveness.

Current as Black Power is the conflict involving Caliban and Prospero. A creature underprivileged and enslaved is taught to think and speak, and promptly turns that training against his mentor, who, for a while, is as patronizing as any modern patrician. Again, the growth of the man Prospero is highlighted by his compassionate freeing of the human soul he has helped advance.

If we are impatient with what seems to be Caliban's ingratitude, we can be sympathetic with his longing for more of the liberty his taste of learning has engendered.

Those jokers, the storm-scared Trinculo and the tipsy Stephano, clown through the island like a pair of drop-out drinking companions, hysterical at their own attempts at humor, and happily taunting the "Moon Calf" (Caliban) as they would a stray pup. Their comedy, low and lugubrious, springs more from their antics than from their wits. It is typical and tell-tale that a splash of glittering garments should divert them from the serious, ugly mission their Monster has in mind.

All these players are but shadows, and the shades, the nymphs, the goddesses, may have been tailored purely for the Court of James the First, but they become the timbre and the tempo of *The Tempest,* and must be fused into the dream-like adventure, as in the memory of miracles rejoicingly recalled. So in this many-splendored, oft-told tale, we tell again of hearts that conquer mind and magic, and seek to tell all magically.

6

Two Viewpoints on the Danish Prince

Somewhere in these pages there should be a presentation of at least two concepts of the same play. Since we will be discussing *Hamlet* in some detail when we tell in a later chapter of televising that play, this chapter seems a good place for those two concepts. The two directing concepts here presented deal with productions that were some six years apart. Because of that time lag, the choice should serve as Exhibit A of how directors change in their thinking, and how they are influenced by current tides of world events, albeit that influence often is subconscious.

As mentioned elsewhere in this book, directors feel the pressure to be relevant, and sometimes strain too many points to make their point. Here in these two concepts it should be clear that straining is not necessary.

Youth's restiveness with the status quo, the generation gap in understanding, the greed of those in power for more power, the high ideals of youth, the search for identity, the verbalizing and procrastinating, the fears, the hopes, the passions—they all are there in Shakespeare's incredible, immortal play. In fact, the relevance of *Hamlet* to our world today is so clear that a director would be hard put not to let it surface.

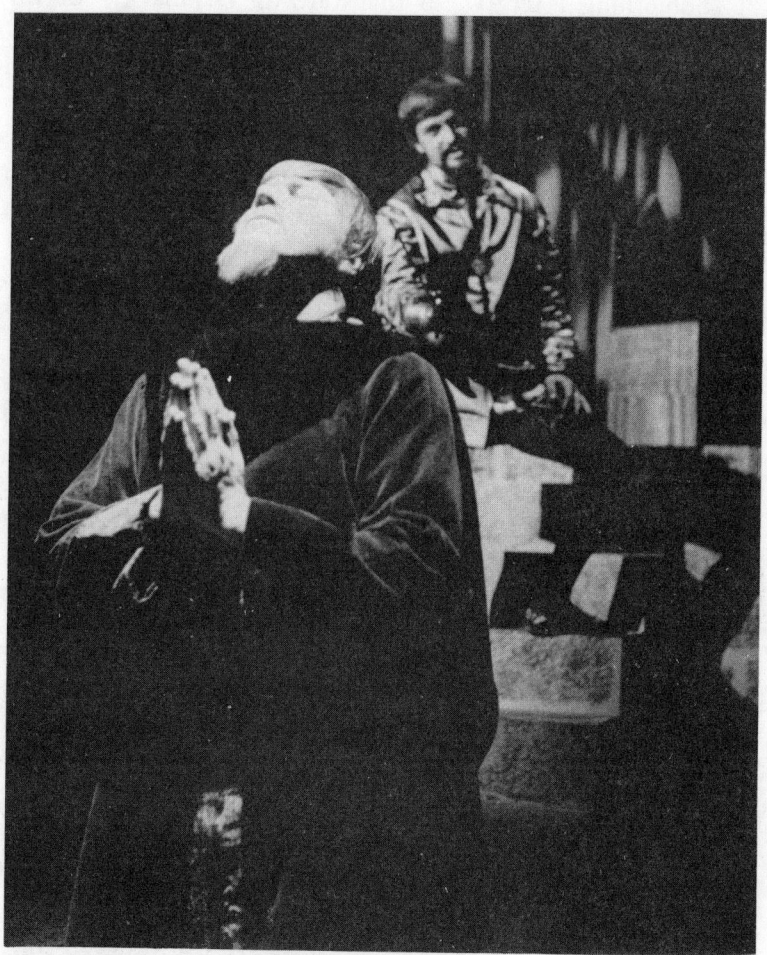

King Claudius and Hamlet, *Hamlet, Prince of Denmark*

Hamlet, Prince of Denmark
DIRECTING CONCEPT ONE

"Something is rotten in the state of Denmark," or one might say "with the state of man." Pit the current world crises against the Christian ideal of nonviolence and Hamlet's problem becomes challengingly contemporary.

The conflict of *Hamlet* centers around a young man's progress toward conscience, concern, and courage. Sudden encounter with suspicion of gross injustice pricks the young

King Claudius and Hamlet, *Hamlet, Prince of Denmark.*
COURTESY PARMENTER STUDIOS

Prince's conscience. Esteem for his father's name and honor, and the emotional shock of his mother's sudden marriage, jolt him into concern. But the courage to involve himself in the violence of revenge comes hard to a sensitive intellectual.

Indeed, involvement does not come readily to Hamlet. From carefree student days at Wittenberg, he is called home to find his world shattered. His mother, whom he loves deeply, has, in the very wake of his father's sudden death, married his uncle, whom he has probably never liked or trusted, who has usurped the throne to which he is the rightful heir, and, to add to his bewilderment, his adored and doting mother seems happy with the present arrangement. It is in the torment of this heartbreak and bewilderment that Hamlet must now meet crisis after crisis. Through the encounter of such crises, a young man must mature or perish. Mores and amity for a "dear father murder'd" indicate clearly that he must avenge the death of the king by ridding the throne of the murderer-usurper.

Conscience calls up the very voice and form of the dead king to involve him in this concept. But only when his mother falls dying, and his friend and he are mortally wounded, and he is reminded "The king's to blame," only then has he courage enough to make the violent thrust that kills his uncle. Of utmost significance is the fact that the act of violence is finally executed by a Hamlet who has grown into the maturity of compassion, compassion that may well symbolize his forgiveness of all who have hurt him, even his uncle, whom he now kills, not so much in anger as out of duty. The young Prince of Denmark has arrived at a peak of nobility, only to crack his own heart and fall to final rest.

Moving in chilly mist, in light and shadow like sunlight

Ophelia, *Hamlet, Prince of Denmark*

in deep forest—moving within sound of pounding surfs and winds that sing with banshee howl, hearing the thunder of impending doom, accented by distant hunter's horn, by martial trumpet flare, drum roll, or pipers playing both gay and doleful tunes, accented by call of birds, and ever the deep-voiced bell of time and the jangling of other bells—the great and lowly of Elsinore, here in this lonely stretch of earth and time, still live in Christendom. Here, in the involvement of hate and love, of violence and vengeance, of foul deeds and noble thoughts, they may move upward, be it ever so slightly, upward from mist to sunlight.

Hamlet, Prince of Denmark

DIRECTING CONCEPT TWO

To tell the familiar Hamlet tale with relevance and excitement, with sharp, stark story line; with strong, clear, character relationships; with bold emotional peaks and depths; with mood of impending doom, but with light as well as shadow; with atmosphere that hints of ancient Elsinore; with style both lyrical and real; with passion, zest, and joy; and with the Bard's compelling urgency and compassion—this is the formidable directing objective.

Prince Hamlet, home from college, mourns his beloved father's recent death and resents his mother's hasty marriage to his uncle, who now wears his father's crown. A lively, witty intellectual with a heart that loves and longs for love, he feels the hurt of loneliness in a shattered world. He aches for reciprocal affection but feels only alienation from those he loves. Queen Gertrude, his mother, speaks gently, pleadingly, but he cannot be sure of one who

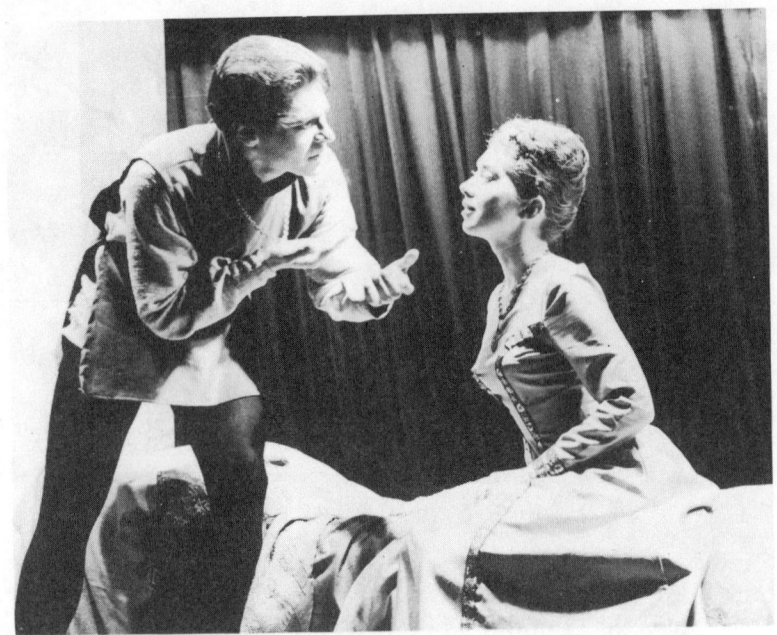

Hamlet and Queen Gertrude, *Hamlet, Prince of Denmark*

so quickly gave her heart again to a second husband, and feels, at best, he is but secondary to his uncle Claudius.

His friend Laertes is warm, but he is off to France, and there is Laertes' sister Ophelia—what of her? What of Ophelia? He did love her once, but will she, can she, return his love? Her father is a meddler, and though Hamlet is fond of the prattling old Polonius, he can neither trust him nor take him seriously. Even Rosencrantz and Guildenstern, old school friends whom he is happy to see, deceive and disappoint him. A man of mind and heart, he finds (as intellectuals often do) that his brilliance only complicates the dictates of his heart. There is, of course, Horatio—good friend and true—and him the Prince will wear in his heart's core till the end.

Two Viewpoints on the Danish Prince

Forthright, outgoing Horatio is as uncomplicated as a young Wittenberg scholar could be, yet he willingly becomes involved in desperate complications.

King Claudius Hamlet cannot trust in spite of his jocose

Hamlet, *Hamlet, Prince of Denmark*

efforts to feign parental fondness, for the nephew he acknowledges is next in line as Denmark's king. Pretender to a throne he came to ruthlessly, the uncle is not easy beneath the crown he wears with too much swagger, but heavier than the crown is the guilt King Claudius bears. Why did he do the awful thing he did? For power? For Gertrude's love? He may not know himself, but having done the deed, he now must live with it in desperate juggling of deceit and skillful skullduggery. He loves his queen and loves his throne and wishes things would settle down to quiet reign, but there is young Hamlet whom he fears, and finds he cannot deftly handle.

He is not taken in by Hamlet's reported madness, but learning that Polonius was killed by Hamlet's sword, which might well have been intended for him, he quickly takes advantage of the madness pitch to hustle Hamlet off to England. His throne and very life are threatened by the enraged Laertes, who returns from France to avenge the death of his father, Polonius. King Claudius cunningly turns the vengeance of Laertes on the real murderer of

Fencing scene, *Hamlet, Prince of Denmark*

Two Viewpoints on the Danish Prince

Polonius, Hamlet, and when the king learns of Hamlet's return to Denmark, presses, with adroit inventiveness, for a match in which Hamlet will be killed in such a way that it will appear as accident.

Gertrude, whose marriage to Claudius may have been for expediency or love or both, is loyal to her son and is disturbed by his despair. His moodiness and strange behavior suggest insanity to her, but after the horror in her chamber and Hamlet's baring of his soul to her, she comes to the awful realization that she is married to the man who killed her first husband. Whatever love she had for Claudius turns to horror and hostility.

Ophelia, the darling of the court, is flattered by Ham-

Claudius, Polonius, Gertrude, Ophelia, *Hamlet, Prince of Denmark*

let's "tenders" to her, accepting his love and falling in love, but hampered in expression of her love because of duty to her father and respect for Laertes' brotherly advice. Her deliberate deception, Hamlet's furious reaction, and her father's death at Hamlet's hand, drive her insane. The poignancy of a love that might have been hangs in echo over the movement of the play. "How should I my true love know?" The song in melody and lyric is the essence of Ophelia's quandary, and the quintessence of Hamlet's quest.

Laertes, dashing man about France, and about Denmark when he is home, has a deep fondness for Hamlet, but Hamlet is a prince and has a longer tether than has Laertes' loving sister; so he must advise her accordingly. Both he and his sister are devoted to each other and to their father, though they share their private good-natured jokes about the garrulous old busybody. A man of fashion, sophistication, and fencing skill, Laertes is formidable, as he proves upon his return to Elsinore to avenge his father's death. Yet, when he learns, at the end, that Claudius has

Players scene, *Hamlet, Prince of Denmark*

tricked him into killing his long-time boyhood friend, he is quick to confess to Hamlet and beg his forgiveness with his dying breath.

More than foolish, prating knave is Polonius. More indeed. He is the King's key man, and his loyalty to the throne is deep and dependable, though it is the throne, more than the man who occupies it, that commands his respect. He is known and liked throughout the court, and probably knows more about the inner workings of state affairs than anyone, including the King. He is fond of Hamlet, having watched him grow up, and is pleased that his daughter is admired by the Prince, but concerned lest Ophelia let herself be wooed too seriously by a man who, after all, will probably marry royalty.

Now the horn sounds, honingly, over that fateful night in Elsinore. The bell beats twelve, the neighboring surf pounds majestically, and a ghost appears to the guards in

Fencing scene, *Hamlet, Prince of Denmark*

the midnight mist. Faintly, ever so faintly, we may hear the minor third, suggesting the haunting calling of Hamlet's name, as later we hear the plaintive echoing and reechoing of Ophelia's song, and again the bells that beat out the hour and toll Ophelia's obsequies.

The misty night gives way to bright merriment in the great hall of Elsinore, and the movement flows on from castle to parapet, to lonely crag and back to castle and chambers of the castle, then out to Ophelia's burial place, and finally home again in the courtyard of Elsinore, as light, shadow, color, and sound weave the magic that is theatre, that is *Hamlet,* that is Shakespeare.

7

What Light from Yonder Window Breaks?

So long as there is love on this lonely little planet there will be Romeos and Juliets. Only those lads with the touch of the poet will see their sweethearts as Romeo saw his Juliet.

"It is the east and Juliet is the sun." Yet love finds the poet in most unlikely places. There is in each of us, when we are in love, at least the longing of the poet, that longing to find words to express deep stirrings inexpressible. The kids don't talk of larks and nightingales, or sigh to be a glove to touch a cheek, not nowadays. They speak a different language now, and talk of skis and motor bikes, and trips and busts, and seem blasé before they're twelve, but let us not be deceived. All such deception was dispelled by youth's almost universal enthusiasm for the filmed *Love Story* and for the film of Zeffirelli's *Romeo and Juliet*.

In Zeffirelli's motion picture of the play, as in the play's first showing long ago in the late sixteenth century, a light broke through a window like a sunburst on a lonely world.

Ever lonely for love, the world breaks into springtime when Juliet speaks, "Sweet, good night! This bud of love, by summer's ripening breath, may prove a beauteous flower when next we meet."

Girls may not speak like that today, but men may wish they could, and men may wish their own tongues could

Romeo and Juliet, *Romeo and Juliet*. COURTESY NBC TELEVISION

say such things as "Sleep dwell upon thine eyes, peace in thy breast. Would I were sleep and peace, so sweet to rest!"

Young love, the theme of *Romeo and Juliet,* returns us to young love, no matter what our age, reminding us that we were born to love and be in love, persuading every living soul to be in love with life. "My bounty is as boundless as the sea, my love as deep; the more I give to thee, the more I have, for both are infinite."

Cannot the world use always such boundless bounty? If only human beings could ever love so infinitely! But even in this lyrical love story, the joy of love must play against the curse of hate.

"Two households, both alike in dignity . . . From ancient grudge, break to new mutiny." Bigotry, suspicion, and blind enmity isolate neighbors from neighbors, nations from nations, and race from race. Hearts will break, blood flow, young lives be lost before grief-stricken fathers will offer their hands in exchange of pardons, and hear their scolding Duke berate them, "A glooming peace this morning with it brings; the sun for sorrow will not show his head. Go hence, to have more talk of these sad things. Some shall be pardon'd, and some punished. For never was a story of more woe than this of Juliet, and her Romeo."

Perhaps this play, more than most plays, affects the players. Young actors in particular seem to get caught up in it. They are bound all through rehearsals in a close community. This fortunate circumstance has its rewards in more ways than the obvious contribution that it makes for good ensemble playing. The strong communal spirit reaches into the wings, embracing all the crews, and what a piece of good luck that turned out to be in one of our productions of the play! The incident is a pertinent comment on the value of teamwork.

It was our opening performance of a lengthy run. The house was packed, the play was going well—so well in fact

Romeo and Juliet, *Romeo and Juliet*

What Light from Yonder Window Breaks?

that fingers were crossed and wood rapped on in hope our luck would hold.

The Prologue, a deep-voiced Black, got things off to an excellent start—the opening street fight went with great excitement, the players all were playing high, free of the usual opening-night jitters, the sound and light cues were right on the button, and the audience was with us every minute. Then, just before we hit the party scene, it happened. A power failure. A circuit breaker? No. A transformer? No. Nothing so simple. A general power failure, plunging that entire section of the city into deep darkness.

The team was on the beam! No panic, no disruption, no fluster anywhere, and most particularly on stage. It hap-

Mercutio, *Romeo and Juliet*

pened in the middle of Romeo's speech. The speech went on. The cue picked up, the dialogue flowed along as though the blackout had been planned. In fact, a planned blackout couldn't have gone better, for almost before the audience was aware of darkness, an actor playing a servant in the play entered with a candle and took position down stage, shielding the taper from the eyes of the audience, and instantly, as if on cue, another servant entered with a candle on the opposite side. Soon other candles appeared, along with torches slated for the final scene, and the stage became a blaze of candlelight. It all seemed more than right for the party scene, a stroke of directorial genius, no less.

Meanwhile, as the play flowed along, telephones were busy. How quickly could the power be restored? The calls brought little satisfaction. An hour, perhaps three quarters, possibly thirty minutes.

The party over, the next scene went on, flowing into the next and the next, the taper-tenders faithfully holding their positions. *Romeo and Juliet* by candle light! Something new. But, please, nobody tell the fire inspector.

Accustomed now to the candlelight, we began to worry about what would happen when the high wattage hit the stage again, jolting us all back into the age of power. Still there were all those beautifully worked-out lighting cues! It was a shame to have them go to waste. The balcony scene was on. The candles and torches gave the lovers a special intimate glow. Horrors! What if the power should pop on in the midst of "Good night, good night. Parting is such sweet sorrow. . . ." The illusion would be shot. Could the operators on the switchboard cut the circuits and hold off in case the power returned, hold off at least until the end of the balcony scene? It would be pretty tricky. In fact, we worried about those lighting people, and about the sound technicians too. Their cues would be all fouled up.

Romeo, *Romeo and Juliet*. COURTESY NBC TELEVISION

"Would I were sleep and peace, so sweet to rest." It's over. The balcony scene is over, and Romeo makes his exit.

Then, suddenly again, as though on cue, the power is on. The spots take over and the candles vanish, and wonder of wonders, those marvelous lighting people in the booth are right on cue. The same is true of sound. All through the power failure they kept their heads and ran their cues on dead equipment by flashlight. Teamwork! Imbued with the spirit of the play, cast and crews weathered the emergency.

Romeo and Juliet
DIRECTING CONCEPT

This side *West Side Story,* the tale of Juliet and her Romeo is extra existentialist. The star-crossed lovers are no longer lost in the romantic mist of Renaissance Verona, but from the hatreds of our nations and our neighborhoods, they capture and engage us in involvement.

Biting the thumb or thumbing the nose, the insolent gesture may be for a Montague or a member of the "wrong," the "other," party, the enemy across the alley or the sea. The immaturity of mature men is not confined to Capulets and Montagues. Youth, nourished in the streets of hate, will starve for love in any age, and denied that love by elders, will rebel and die, when lonely longing leads only to futility.

What Light from Yonder Window Breaks? 103

This is a current cry, this cry of Romeo and Juliet for love. This is a cry of young aching hearts amidst the madness of indifference and moral impotence, a cry of passionate innocence against paranoic guilt, a cry, a pang, a paean

Juliet and Romeo, *Romeo and Juliet.* COURTESY TAVIAN

for the right to live and love, to freely choose to taste the idyllic fruit and know the touch of heart to heart, and even more, the reach of soul for soul.

Even the lusty youths, singing through the streets in quest of damsels to embrace, are on fire, not so much with lust as love of life, and they will thrust impetuous swords, not so much to kill or die as to defy that authority that traps them in a strange, inviolate, honor code of hate.

Juliet, the wonder of womanhood waking within her, will "look to like" in fillial obedience, but when the strangeness of a stranger's wanting kiss stirs want in her, she will rebel against parental tyranny, a tyranny based not on love, but stubborn will to have their child submit to wishes of their own frustrated lives. She will rebel, as will a modern

Benvolio, Nurse, and Peter, *Romeo and Juliet*

girl, be she fourteen or twenty, unloved at home and longing for love, and when her last friend ends her last hope, bidding her conform, she will seek desperate means to consummate her ends.

So Juliet, moving through the mist of night, fearful of the lark who heralds day, is all romance, and all the women who ever risk romance.

This is a night-time play, with street brawls in the dark, with moonlight serenades, clandestine meetings with a Friar, and in the end, the tomb, which is the last, long night. Morning and daylight are but the fleeting sound of horns against the lush, rich sigh of strings and ebullient clarionets.

Striding through the night, feeling his manhood, yet feeling his need to prove his manhood, is Romeo, virile and vital, with the verve of life. Reveling in the ribaldry of Mercutio, singing with his cohorts, he knows that song and sex are not enough to stay the hungers of a heart that longs to fill the longing of another heart. In reckless candor, he will crash the party of the family enemy, vault the enemy wall, and slay the slayer of his friend, though only a moment since, he would have befriended the slayer, loving him as kin, his love for Juliet having exalted him above all hate. Then, remorseful of his heinous sin, and more remorseful for the hurt his deed has brought to his Juliet, he would erase his name by stabbing out his life, but for the chance to see his beloved once again before his banishment.

It is the banishment of lover from beloved that young love cannot bear. Impetuous and impatient youth cannot wait for time when time is but the certain separation fraught with time's uncertainty. "Banishéd." That one word, "Banishéd," is the bodkin blow, unbearable.

Mantua is a million miles from her whom he loves, but

when he hears, erroneously, that she is dead, he leaps the miles to beat his way to Juliet's tomb, beating to death the unfortunate Paris who would apprehend him, then tender-

Juliet and Nurse, *Romeo and Juliet*

What Light from Yonder Window Breaks? 107

ing tenderness to Paris, remembering that he loved his love.

Now, in the irony of death, and waking to take death, echoes the fatal dirge of futility, the dirge for all who accept futility as final, never knowing the alternative, which may be but a breath away.

The night is over, and, in the shadows of the dawn, the sorrowing neighbors stand, their old and foolish enmity burned out at last, as the light of clemency burns into their hearts.

"Some will be pardoned, some punished." Forgiveness of himself will be hard for the generous, ministrative Friar. The humor-loving, garrulous, well-meaning nurse will find now that humor comes hard, when she remembers what she might have said, when she said "I think it best you marry

Romeo and Juliet, *Romeo and Juliet*

with the County." Faithful Benvolio will not sing again with Romeo and Mercutio, and the lonely Montagues will know loneliness known only by the Capulets.

Lady Capulet and Juliet, *Romeo and Juliet*

What Light from Yonder Window Breaks? 109

So, from the misty nights of old Verona, memories melt into the nights of now, and we are left darkling, seeking the light of love.

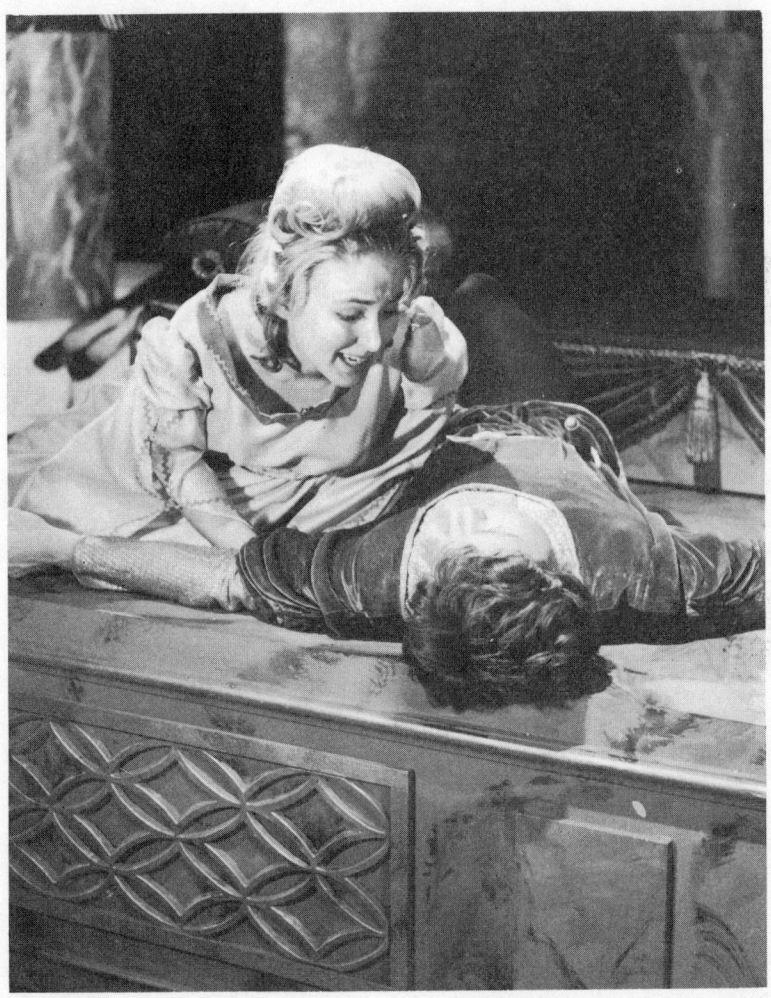

Juliet and Romeo, *Romeo and Juliet.* COURTESY NBC TELEVISION

The light will filter fleetingly through orchard branches, garden walls, cloister casements, bursting at times into the radiant ecstasy that was the Italy of the fifteenth century, melting anon from gold of afternoon to silver of the starlit night, the light and shadow in themselves telling of a time of saints and devils, a time of beauty and of violence.

Rich colors of scarlet and gold, azure and burgundy, flow in the free simplicity of the period style, against classic mass and form of rose-tinted marble, as action flows with equal freedom from street to suite, to garden, cloister, boudoir, or wheresoever we needs must be to live the story.

In the story the flowering of the Renaissance is reflected, not the Renaissance of intellect alone, but the reawakening of awareness, expressed in the full gamut of emotions, for in the story, as in the century of its settings, horrendous deeds of hate hint of the deeds of Cesare Borgia, while words of pure beauty, echoing from the balcony of Juliet, suggest angelic gifts from Fra Angelico.

8
From Stage to Camera with the Bard

The foregoing production concepts are for plays that we have directed for the stage. The Shakespearean plays that we have prepared for television differ, not in basic concept, but in the execution of the concept. We find the difference so fascinating that we think it will be of special interest to readers of this book. Shaping Shakespeare to a TV time slot is a challenge with many ramifications. Some of those ramifications may be enlightening. Others are decidedly funny.

The sad thing about the funny incidents is that they were meant to be quite serious, but mishaps do occur, and when they are amusing, they may as well be shared.

Certainly the death of Antony in *Antony and Cleopatra* is a sobering moment, but when the camera holds on the dead Antony instead of panning to a close-up of Cleopatra, and when the actor playing Antony, thinking himself to be off camera, opens one eye and wiggles for all the viewers to see, the illusion is somewhat shattered. Cameramen are sometimes slow to pick up cues. Actors also forget to count. Antony should have counted ten before he moved, to give the camera time to cut to Cleopatra. He didn't.

In a telecast of *Romeo and Juliet,* Juliet counted, but she still got caught. Following the moment when the nurse discovers her in a trance and presumably dead, the camera was supposed to stay on the nurse and follow her as she ran down stairs. Instead, it stayed on Juliet, who, thinking she was off camera, after her ten count popped out of bed and scrambled down the escape ladder, blithely unaware that she was causing hysterics or bewilderment among thousands of viewers.

She learned later, and vied with the cameraman for the Blooper Award. That was not our prize-winning television

Burbank Studio, *Romeo and Juliet.* COURTESY NBC TELEVISION

production of *Romeo and Juliet*—memorable it was, but not prize winning. Another time, we did much better.

Another time, however, we did not fare well, when Petruchio in *The Taming of the Shrew* failed to observe a cut, adding a good two miuntes to the play, minutes for which we had to compensate by speeding up the final scene, forcing Katharine to lose her well-rehearsed subtleties in her celebrated final speech.

In another play a scene was added at the last minute to clarify the exposition. Again the timing had to be accounted for, and the carefully rehearsed tempos adjusted to the sweep hand on the studio clock. That was not funny, but the lights and mikes on the opening of the added scene failed to come up on cue, and that, at least in retrospect, was. Retrospect often works wonders with the sense of humor. And it should be pointed out that these productions were a feature of experimental education television, and not our network shows.

At those times when a good laugh seems the best way to lick one's wounds, it is comforting to remember that Shakespeare, too, had a saving sense of humor.

Adapting Shakespeare to camera is a good deal more than tailoring the script. Directors steeped in the stage tradition are in strange country there among all those sets strung around the perimeter of the studio. Actors so trained are equally alien. The adjustments are staggering. Playgoers, play readers, and people familiar only with the tube side of television usually find the studio side of the production quite as entertaining as the play itself. Let us describe a little of what happens.

Come with us now to one of the largest television studios in the world. It is in Burbank, California. You are about to witness the transfer of a stage production to the air. It is a process that would no doubt have fascinated Shakespeare, especially since it is his *Hamlet* that we are to transfer.

Romeo, *Romeo and Juliet*

From Stage to Camera with the Bard 115

Is that bust on the shelf scowling at us? We wondered about that and worried at first, but as we thought the matter through, we remembered that Shakespeare was a craftsman as well as a poet. As craftsman he wrote "to spec," the specifications being the limitations of the theatres of his time. If he had had to contend with the limitations of cameras, microphones, and time slots, he would have met the challenge, or so it seems to us, and his poetry would have transcended, as it always does. So the indestructible *Hamlet, Prince of Denmark* experiences another transmigration.

At a quarter of eight on a fine June morning we are in the mammoth studios of the National Broadcasting Company (KNBC) in Burbank. Our call is for 8:00 A.M. We step into Studio B, a breathtaking experience, this being the largest TV studio in the nation. There are our sets, fabulous and beautiful, awaiting our use.

Backed by the enthusiastic support of studio top brass, excited over doing the first college *Hamlet,* the first Shakespearean telecast to emanate from Hollywood, the first Shakespearean telecast in color to come out of the West, and the biggest dramatic show ever to have originated at KNBC, the art director has gone all out. So there they are, our six sets strung along the walls of the studio which, in its immensity, measures 120 feet in length, 85 feet in width, and some 70 feet to the grid work above, from which hangs a myriad of drops, floodlights, and the like. To our right is the parapet where the play will open and which will later become the churchyard for Ophelia's funeral. Workmen, who have been on duty all night, are just finishing. Across from the parapet, against the far-distant wall, is the throne room. We journey over to try the thrones of the King and Queen. Our feet dangle, but crimson-carpeted steps move into place beneath our feet and we are monarchs of all we survey—the TV director, the production manager, the stage manager, some of the technicians, and the rest of our *Hamlet* company arriving on schedule.

This is that long-awaited day. In about thirteen hours, we will tape the show for release on the following Sunday. The hours ahead are to be filled with wonder, excitement, and hard work. But not all the work had been left until this final day—not by a long shot. Last night the *Hamlet* company rehearsed in one of the larger studios at Hollywood and Vine from seven until eleven, and prior to that, two twelve-hour rehearsals were held on campus—two, that is,

Juliet, *Romeo and Juliet*

engaging the TV director. We conducted other TV rehearsals of the production, which had played some ten performances prior to the TV scheduling.

At the first rehearsal conducted by the TV director, the time was spent in scaling the actors down from stage to camera, getting them to speak in a conversational manner, to curtail their gestures, to speak and listen with their eyes, and to restrain their facial expressions.

"Don't worry," said the TV director to us, aware of our concern about the seeming loss of the Shakespearean style. "First," he explained, "we trim them to size, tube size, then we will scale them up to Shakespeare again." He did, after he had seen them through the camera blocking.

The camera blocking was roughed in on the campus stage, each set chalked on the floor, and rehearsing proceeded with the actors keeping camera positions always in mind.

In mind, too, were the cuts that had to be observed. From a two-and-a-half-hour show, the script had to be trimmed down to a sixty-minute slot, which meant about fifty-seven minutes' actual playing time. The cutting was made by hewing to the story line, but all characters were retained who were in the stage production, and many of the purple patches were salvaged, though only as they enriched character or developed conflict and never for themselves alone.

While actors were setting their new blocking, adjusting to the streamlined version, unlearning much of what they had memorized for the stage production, the prop and costume people were having their problems. Fake swords and crowns that appeared thoroughly convincing on stage simply would not pass under the close scrutiny of the camera. The camera calls for the real McCoy. Costumes, too, that were beautiful on stage would not, in some cases, be right for color television. The vacuum tubes of the color camera are critically selective and respond best to certain

Lady Capulet and Juliet, *Romeo and Juliet*

hues and tones. The use of blacks and whites must be done with great caution, since either color too near the face of an actor causes him to appear as though head were detached from body.

All these adjustments are, at long last, behind us now, as we begin work on the day of the taping. The director calls the cast, explains that he wants first to walk them through the show to get them familiar with the sets. This he does, taking time to change or adjust business to make the best use of the settings. Then at 10:00 A.M. the camera crew arrives, the cast is again put through the show, and now the imagination of the director is put to the test as he learns very quickly where he has envisioned shots wisely, and where he has missed. Inevitably shots have to be adjusted, camera positions altered, business tightened, but on the whole, the blocking proves to be excellent, and we are ready now for lights.

A break for lunch, and the cast returns to walk through once more for the lighting crew. No dialogue this time through, but all movement and all picturizations are important, and again adjustments must be made.

Now it is three in the afternoon, and the beehive has been buzzing since before eight, many, including the director, not even stopping for lunch, or munching one of the sandwiches brought in while they went on working. Three o'clock and the call comes, "Report to make-up."

Back in the make-up rooms, down the corridor lined with dressing rooms, make-up artists alter faces. Make-up for color TV differs from make-up for black and white productions in that it is much lighter and is applied very much as street make-up, except for the character make-ups.

While some are being made up, others are getting into costume, and still others are called to the set by the director, who wants to put a final finish on a certain scene or run through certain sections to set sound levels.

Dress rehearsal is set for four-thirty, but it is five by

Friar Laurence and Romeo, *Romeo and Juliet*

the time all technical items are checked, and we are now, finally, in the final, now-or-never stage. This is a dress with stops, since final adjustments are inevitable. With the cast on the floor are the stage manager, his assistant, three cameramen, their assistants, two boom men, two or three prop men, half a dozen electricians, a crew of stage hands, one or two from wardrobe, one of the two make-up artists popping in to take a look, the producer, and the production manager, who, along with the producer, moves about from floor to control booth and into the sponsor's booth to catch the show from various angles.

In the booth are the director, the video engineer, the audio engineer, and their assistants. In all, some twenty-five to thirty persons, exclusive of the cast, are engaged in readying the show for the air, and they will be on duty and engaged until the show is safely taped.

It is seven-fifty when we finish the dress rehearsal. Now, "Everybody to make-up for a final powdering. Be back in the studio for countdown at eight-ten," comes the director's call over the intercom. While players scamper for final costume adjustments, to check on hand props, or to get a drink of water and take a deep gulp of breath, the technical crews take a breather if they're lucky, but many of the crews have, themselves, last-minute items to check. Certainly the director, who has not stopped all day, has final matters to check, and he will be checking them right up to air time.

"Ten seconds—five—three—two—" Horn theme, and the show is on. Can they do it? Can they possibly run this thing through without a blooper, without a flub? Any one, any dozen of a hundred things could go wrong. A boom man, lifting a mike just a little late, can throw a shadow on the cyc. A camera man, just a trifle off course, can be out of focus. Will the props get on? Will the gain on the mikes be right to pick up the soft passages? Will Props remember to put a paper napkin in the bottom of the goblet, which resounded with a loud "ping" when the king

Final scene, *Romeo and Juliet*

dropped the pearl in it during dress rehearsal?

The technicians are professional and know their business, but they seemed pretty casual during rehearsal. It's all in a day's work. But is it? No. Not *Hamlet*. This is something special, and they are all dead serious. Every man, every mind is on the show. These are the studio's top experts. Even so, can it go without a slip?

Will the tension hold, or break? In the sponsors' booth we watch the color screen alongside another screen showing the image in black and white. The general manager himself has come to watch. So far, perfect—not a slip. These experts are expert, but they are working with college players. But the college actors have rehearsed far, far more than have the staff of experts on this show.

"Good night, sweet Prince. . . ." Horatio is in his final speech. Hold, hold that final freeze, hold for the credits' crawl. You're still on camera.

"NBC has been proud to present, in color. . . ." He's saying it—the announcer is on the sign-off. It's over. Not a fluff, not a flub—it's over, and on the floor of the huge studio the crews, to a man, are applauding. They were expecting retakes. Inevitable, they thought. But the "kids" did it, and old professionals, recognizing professional attitude when they see it, are congratulating students and one another in that special camaraderie common to backstage and studio alike when the show they have all created clicks.

To win an accolade is always as humbling as it is gratifying. To win ovation from hard-bitten pros was very sobering. *Hamlet* had clicked. The performance went without a hitch, the crews went all out to give beyond the normal call of duty, the head cameraman showing genius in his sensitive response to crucial, definitive shots, the lighting director calling cues to make each climax moment memorable, all working as though the spirit of the Bard himself were in command.

But was that spirit there, and were we being true to it? The vital aspect of that question was the latter half. Had we been faithful to Shakespeare's intent? We meant to be, we have always meant to be, but who can say for certain what his intent was, really, or, even more to the point, what it would be today were he encountered with our modern wonders and the miracle of television?

The question has recurred in subsequent telecasts of other Shakespeare plays. What would he do with this fabulous, monstrous medium? What would he do, standing where we now stand on the threshold of invention that will put all that has been done in deep shadow? The time of video cassettes is now at hand, and that could mean that the classics could come to every school, to every home. A video tape or film, mere pocket size, can bring to any TV tube either the best or the most degenerate of all our civil-

Juliet, *Romeo and Juliet*. COURTESY NBC TELEVISION

ization has to offer. That prospect is staggering, and, at the same time, stimulating.

Now that the laser ray has made conventional photography all but obsolete, the wonders presently at hand are catastrophic. What will we do with holograms, the three-dimensional pictures now at hand? What would a Shakespeare do with such devices?

"There are more things in heaven and earth, Horatio, than are dreamt of in your philosophy." Four centuries pass, and we still reach for things in heaven and earth, and heaven and earth still mete out marvels. Some of those marvels are discoveries belonging to modernity. Some of those marvels are yet to be rediscovered in the plays of Shakespeare. In book, on stage, on screen, on tube, on tape, the rediscovering continues.

To find a colloquy of fellows in a television studio rediscovering *Hamlet* matched most favorably the prospect of discovery the million viewers might experience.

Thanks to that colloquy, and to electronic marvels, *Hamlet, Prince of Denmark* would play to more people in a single night than it ever did throughout the life span of William Shakespeare. Millions would pause to think again, "What a piece of work is a man," and through such thoughts projected through the ages, might think, at least subconsciously, the exalting, self-awakening thoughts of Shakespeare, and take upon themselves "the mystery of things, as though we were God's spies."

9
Genius:
Genes or Hard Knocks?

William Shakespeare: Was he one man or many men? Lest we should be "in manifest danger not to understand him," let us further attempt to take the measure of the man. Was he a man or only a myth? Was Shakespeare merely a name under which various writers wrote, or perhaps one other writer who wished to conceal his identity?

Slaves of erudition, busy with their busy work, seek proof that he was Sir Francis Bacon, or the Earl of Essex, or the Earl of this or the Lord of that, or even, heaven help us, Christopher Marlowe.

Perhaps it is not surprising that limited, unimaginative, pedestrian minds cannot conceive of a genius such as Shakespeare. Such genius, such prolific output are staggering to the average credibility quotient. To those of us who pale at the call to excellence, it is comforting to accept the myth that Shakespeare was actually many men, a staff of writers such as it usually takes to turn out a film script.

The trouble with the staff conjecture is that all members

of it would have had to be theatre craftsmen of the stature of Kit Marlowe, and even his craftsmanship would have had to improve considerably after his memorable *Doctor Faustus* and *The Duchess of Malfi*. Of course the notion that Marlowe was not really killed in that fateful tavern brawl is romantic, as is the thought that he may have escaped to continue writing sub rosa. But suddenly to write with the skill of a Shakespeare? It is not surprising that that idea was never taken very seriously. Nor are the other aspects of the myth taken with much credibility, though, in a sense, it is certainly true that Shakespeare was many men.

Man and boy, he was teacher, actor, poet, playwright, philosopher, businessman, prophet, land owner, lover, husband, parent, and proud owner of a coat of arms. He was thinker, humorist, psychologist, historian, scientist, and mystic.

He was a favorite of the queen and many lords and ladies, a friend of the people, and a loyal colleague in the theatre circle. His competitor, the scholarly Ben Jonson, said that he had "small Latin, and less Greek," but he obviously knew history and the literature of his time, and seemed well abreast of current affairs. As actor he must have had to dance and sing, and use a sword with contemporary skill. He was, in short, a Renaissance man, this man who was many men.

"Let no man blame his son for learning history from Shakespeare." Samuel Taylor Coleridge said that well over a hundred and fifty years ago. History teachers may disagree, but can they account for youth's waning interest in history in recent years? Maybe excessive insistence on authenticity drained the romance from the happenings of the past. Maybe a little romance would restore some ardor for history. Shakespeare's history may not be accurate in every detail, but it is exciting. It is exciting because it deals with people, not mere dates.

Those people, those kings and queens, those lords and ladies, those clowns, those common people make of the past a living present. Their long parade through the centuries has served to link the generations, showing mankind where man has been, hinting at where he yet may go if he is wise enough to avoid ancestral follies. Is that not, after all, the function of history?

We who know those people of the plays, and our number is legion, know them as old friends, friends for whom our affection is an ever-growing thing. We greet them on the stage or on the page with floods of memories and fresh anticipations, experiencing the warmth we often feel at family or class reunions. Katharine, Petruchio, Portia, Bassanio, old Shylock and his Jessica, Ariel and Prospero, Macbeth, his lady, and those witches, Puck, Titania and Oberon, Ophelia, Gertrude, Horatio and Hamlet, the Capulets and Montagues, and Juliet and Romeo, all friends who wander often in the minds of all who have the rare good fortune to know such fascinating people. A man's son, a woman's daughter could fill their minds with much worse things. We needs must whisper thanks across the shoulder.

Against the regimentation of computers and the numbers game, we need the comfort and the challenge of such friends. Too easily we lose our sense of wonder. There in that wonder world we reach for truth. Here, among the friends the bard has given us, we live a while in the indispensable renewal of life. Always we can pick up the text or await the rising curtain with newly kindled wonder. What will our friends be like this time?

Ellen Terry, that darling of the British stage in the

late last century, did her share of wondering. She said she had five different approaches to the role of Portia, and the one she liked best was not the one her public favored. She used to wonder if there had ever been a dramatist whose roles admitted to as many different interpretations as those created by the Shakespeare genius.

"Times change," the star of Sir Henry Irving's theatre admitted, "and parts have to be acted differently for different generations."

Not every role of every dramatist has such dimension. We must admit few do compare with those of Shakespeare. Miss Terry believed that an actress should return at least every ten years to a Shakespearean role previously performed. An actor or an actress would, Miss Terry felt certain, find in the role new life to match his maturation.

Contemporary veterans of Shakespearean roles, such as Sir John Gielgud, Sir Ralph Richardson, and Lord Olivier support the contention of Ellen Terry. They, like others with remarkable careers, return to roles always to discover that they are in strange country. The name is familiar but the character is a brand new game. On and on the exploration goes for actors, directors, playgoers, and readers. Prospero may drown his book of magic, but the character of Prospero, like all the other characters of Shakespeare, bobs back to surface to swim the endless stream of our literary continuum.

Tell us, gentle Will, how did you do it? How did you conceive characters who appear to be utterly unplumbable? How did you write such poetry, such plays as to move millions around the world, and continue to move them after nearly four centuries? How?

If we can find out how, we might pass on the information, hoping somewhere, sometime, to spark another Shakespeare; or, if that sounds too audacious, we might at least spark something in even the least of us to perk up the pituitary glands and generate a little more creative action. Genius is still a baffler, one of our unsolved mysteries. Where does it come from, this thing called genius?

How did a lad from a river town in Warwickshire manage to make it big in London? Genes, perhaps. Could the genes of a simple country girl named Mary fuse so furiously with the genes of a tanner named John? Neither of them, so far as is known, and none of their ancestors, were poets, or playwrights, or even actors.

Plays they may have seen occasionally when traveling troupes came out from London to perform in the inn yard, or when Will's school presented a play in Latin. It is not unlikely that Will himself got his first bite from the theatre bug by playing in such plays, and when a traveling company came to town, he may have been the lad in the front row, or the one who hung around back stage, hounding the actors with a thousand questions.

In any event it is safe to surmise that, sometime in youth, he heard the cry of players, and found himself indubitably stagestruck. But what was the good of being stagestruck in Stratford, a little hick town filled with weavers, tailors, wool merchants, shoemakers, skinners, collar makers, brewers, bakers, pewterers, grocers, coopers, mercers, fishermen, and farmers?

True, there were fish to catch in the Avon, farmers to ferry for a twopence, squirrels to hunt, rabbits to chase, trees to climb, and girls to tease, and mischief enough at school for fun. But what, a boy might wonder, were things like in London?

The smell of the pub, the smell of the church, the smell of the blacksmith shop and of horses mingled with the nostalgic scent of neighboring orchards radiant with bloom in spring, pungent with fruit in summer. The feel of rain, the warmth of sun, the sounds of rattling carts, of boisterous youths, of giggling girls, were all in a day's doings along the quiet Avon. There were things to think about at school, chores to do at home, friends to meet, games to win, events enough to fill the days, but none of it was London, none of it was theatre.

Later there was that girl, Ann Hathaway. What would it be like to romp the fields and woods with her? A chase in the cornfield—love in the rye—"It was a lover and his lass, with a hey and a ho and a hey." "Shall I compare thee to a summer's day?"

She wasn't like the silly sisters of his pals. She was older than Will, eight years at least. What did that matter? At sixteen, he was a man, man enough to go with Ann to find a rector who made them man and wife. Is that how geniuses get started? We're groping for a clue. Did matrimonial bliss augment the D.N.A. of genes? Did Ann bring out the poetry in Will?

Or was matrimony a frustrating trap from which he must one day escape? How did he feel about the two daughters Ann bore him, and the one son? A son was something—an heir to bear his name. What grief, what anguish did he suffer when that son died while still a lad? Is it of such "slings and arrows of outrageous fortune" that genius is born?

Before that tragedy would come about, he would see London. He would quit his teaching job in Stratford and have a taste of London. He would leave quite unexpectedly! Someone went deer poaching on Lord Lucy's neighboring estate. Was it that harum scarum Willy Shakespeare? The sheriff would find out, and guilty or not, Will perhaps found the incident an excuse to clear out and head for London, that city of his dreams.

It was not much of a city in the late sixteenth century, not a city at all by later standards—a lot of wooden buildings among the fields on the banks of the Thames, but the palace of the queen was there, and handsome estates boasting courtyards and great halls where players frequently performed, and there was the Tower, of course, built by Julius Caesar before the fall of Rome.

What young Shakespeare found in London town must have dazzled his stagestruck mind. The town was hot with the plays and players performing in the inn yards of The Bull, The Boar, The Red Lion, and other lively spots, and what was an even greater wonder to behold was The Theatre, a wooden structure, crudely built by an actor named James Burbage, who, in order to escape the constant badgering of players by the Lord High Chamberlain, leased a field on the outskirts, where he opened his place for business some ten years before Shakespeare arrived.

James Burbage had a son named Richard, who would later become a cohort of Shakespeare, but did the enterprising James have a big, fat role waiting for young Will? Was all London waiting with bated breath for the boy wonder from Stratford? Not likely. No doubt his genius had to take the kicks and knocks most tyros take when they tackle the big time. Is this, then, another clue—the taking of the kicks and knocks? The behaviorists and environmentalists may have at each other over this, but it was some years before the name of William Shakespeare surfaced in the theatre-gossip circles of London.

One thing is certain. Shakespeare must have found the competition tough. The actors were of a long line of performers stretching back two and three centuries to the cycle plays and to the Italian commedia dell'arte. They were a rough, hard-bitten lot, skilled in the arts of singing, dancing, and swordplay, quite as much as acting. They knew they had to get the attention of a crowd before they could entertain it. In that art, too, they were highly skilled.

As to the writers of plays, they were university-trained for the most part, and what chance did a bumpkin from up-country have with university wits? Probably he didn't even speak their kind of English. Will must have suffered more than his share of shuns, snubs, and put-downs, which, some would say, is curriculum for the course for those determined to make it.

Still, it was a good time for a young talent to be in London. The town was teeming with adventure. The good Queen Bess, though growing old, defied her age, engaging in scandalous flirtations, and heaping favors upon her favorites. England was competing hard with Spain for the riches of the new-found western world, and there was the constant threat of invasion, a threat that became a close call in 1588 when the mighty Spanish Armada sailed into the English channel, only to be sent limping home by the Queen's good Britons.

Still the warring went on with both Spain and France, causing Elizabeth and all her court constant anxiety. Yet wars and intrigues did not stop adventure. Such men as Drake and Raleigh carried out their expeditions to the New World, and seeds of an empire were scattered with the distant winds.

It was a time of reawakening. The Renaissance came late to England, and Shakespeare rode its crest. There are those who go so far as to say Shakespeare was the English Renaissance, but sober consideration usually leads to the conclusion that giants who lead such movements, giants like

Leonardo da Vinci and Michelangelo, are backed by many kindred minds. Still, in those years of Elizabeth the First, a renaissance was going on and Will was at its vertex.

Long before achievement of artistic recognition and the financial success that accompanied it, there were things the growing genius had to learn. He had to learn that entertaining in the town of London was an intricate business. One must be wanted by nobility before appearing in court or manors of the lords, but even being wanted was of no value until one secured a permit from the city authorities, namely the office of the Lord Chamberlain. Securing the permit was especially hard because the authorities thought that crowds gathered for entertainment were likely to cause riots and exacerbate the spreading of contagions.

Fear of the plague was ever an obsession. That fear caused many a troupe of players to cut short a booking and take to the road. A licensing system, primarily controlled by the Master of Revels, was devised, but licenses, often dealt out as favors, took skillful wangling, quite task enough to turn an artist into a businessman. Getting a toehold meant learning to deal with people, and, even more basic, knowing who were the right people with whom to deal.

Shakespeare's contact with the Burbages was no doubt helpful, as was his early acquaintance with Edward Allen, who was considered the greatest actor of his time. Young Will must have had a zest and amiability that won him favor with men of the profession, and he was no doubt quick to profit from such fraternity.

Being an actor in London was a far cry from the teaching job he left in Stratford and probably much less remunerative. He may have had some homesick pangs. A man gets lonely when the going is rough. Although he was probably much too busy for self pity or much indulgence in nostalgia, he must have wondered some about his wife and children. Ann may have been a scold, a shrew, a perfect model for Baptista's Kate, still, she was his wife, and "Love is not love which alters when it alteration finds"; and even if he were himself a swaggering young Petruchio having his way with London women, he surely had his days of gloom, discouragement, and despair. He must have suffered doubts, suffered moments of remorse, suffered "the thousand natural shocks that flesh is heir to," else he could not have known the suffering of the men and women he created. There he was, trying to make his way, trying to prove himself, gambling his family against an uncertain career. Even so, he was not the last ambitious young man to suffer qualms about his home and family, and nagging doubts about a precarious career.

What kept him, then, in London? What held him to his course? Ambition? Determination? A sense of destiny? Whatever it was, it probably has something to do with our search for clues to genius.

Those character traits that held him to his course saw him through trying times with playwrights Kyd, Peele, and Greene, and later with Marlowe and Jonson. From them he learned the craft of play making, a craft he emulated in his first attempts. There is significance in the fact that he did not imitate them long. Something in his nature led him to develop a technique of his own, a technique that enabled him to write plays that were infinitely beyond anything his colleagues ever achieved.

Doggedly, patiently, deliberately, he acquired the mastery of his medium, but for him the medium was not the message, though he clearly felt that the medium should have message. The message was his great-hearted grasp on life.

For him, life, every minute of it, was a marvelous, exciting adventure, a thing divine given to man, the individual. His message was always for man, the individual.

With all his growing awareness, all his technical growth, Shakespeare was becoming more and more conscious of England—her past, her present, and her future. He hungered to know the nature of his England, to feel the pulsebeat of her dynamic present, to take to his heart the impact of her impressive history, and to catch a vision of her expanding potential.

The blood of an Englishman was surging in the veins of gentle Will, and we shall miss a clue to his genius if we do not pay it heed. In our time nationalism is in some disfavor, but we are dealing with a time when the emerging of nations was an aspect of the human march. He was an Englishman, our universal Will. Now he belongs to the world, but in his time he thought little of such things, and wanted only to be a strong and faithful projector of the English thrust. It happened that that thrust went far beyond the shores of "this little Eden—this demi-paradise—this happy land—this England."

A great and fascinating mind was expanding. To his formal, if provincial education in Stratford, Shakespeare could now add the new translations of Plutarch, and, of more immediate importance, Holinshed's *Chronicles of English History,* a rich source for script material. Florio was translating Montaigne, and Italian and French romances were finding their way into England, and in them were the seeds of such plays as *Measure for Measure, Othello, The Taming of the Shrew,* and *Romeo and Juliet.* Shakespeare was tapping every source, not neglecting the embryo English novelists from whom came germs of *As You Like It* and *A Winter's Tale.* Furthermore, for nearly a hundred years the riches of the Italian Renaissance culture had been pouring into England, and the alert, receptive mind of Shakespeare was a ready, bottomless vessel.

As Margaret Webster says in her *Shakespeare without Tears,* "Shakespeare found the instruments of immortality ready to his hand."

Therein lies another key to his genius. An alert, sensitive, responsive mind, a mind that can select essentials and discard chaff, that can see those essentials in perspective and arrange them into an artistic whole, that kind of mind does seem to be something of a requisite. To the genes, then, must be added the impact of environment and the accumulation of knowledge.

To the genes, too, must be added many, many intangibles, intangibles about which we can only speculate, but in our quest for clues of genius, surely a little speculation is permissible.

History tells us so little about William Shakespeare that we must read his life into that part of him that is immortal. His plays tell us much. They tell of his compassion, his courage, his confidence, his great-hearted acceptance of life, his awareness of good and evil, and his belief in the essential goodness of human beings. Alas, they do not tell us how he got to be a genius. Yet, perhaps implicitly, they do shed light.

There is light on the subject in the very dimension of his character. A lesser writer, or one less careful, could not have created characters with such diverse potentials. Portia, as Miss Terry said, can be played in many ways and still be Portia. The same may be said of Shylock and all the other characters in *The Merchant of Venice,* and of virtually all the characters in all the Shakespearean plays.

Is Hamlet mad, or only feigning madness? Is Iago all villain or is there some justification for his treachery? Is Macbeth a mere tool in the hands of his ambitious wife, or does he have a will of his own? Is Katharine nothing but a shrew, or is there a charge of electric current that draws Petruchio and her together, and does she, in the end, out-fox her conqueror? Corresponding questions can be asked of nearly every character Shakespeare created, questions that are asked repeatedly by actors and directors.

Such careful creativity may be purely the product of intuition, or it may be the result of meticulous craftsmanship. If it was the former, then the gift was there from the beginning, a gift of heaven, heredity, or DNA. If it was the latter, we must give credit to a growth, a trace of progress, a willed effort to improve. How does one get to be a genius? Hard work helps. Thousands of gifted people fade into oblivion each year for want of work and self discipline. Shakespeare may have been the favored son of Taurus, blessed by the stars, or by St. George on whose birthday he allegedly was born, but what might have happened if he had never gone to London, and had not reached for goals unreachable?

Or suppose he had rested on the laurels of his first success. He could have quit midway and gone home to Ann and Stratford. By all accounts his earnings would have afforded him such retirement. He was wealthy enough to purchase a sizable estate in Warwickshire some years before he took his final leave of London. Why should he have wanted to go on working? More to the point, why should he have wanted to go on growing? Is that another mark of genius?

Scholars and analysts who know about such things declare a drastic difference between a play like *The Comedy of Errors,* one of his first, and *The Tempest,* thought to have been his last. Almost anyone who reads the early plays and compares them to his later works sees evidence of growth. Much of that growth may have been due at first to competition. Survival in the theatre in any age is rough going. Still, judging from the extant plays of his competitors, he soon outstripped them in artistry and probably in popularity as well, because the Elizabethan audiences were as quick as any to give support to superior entertainment.

Besides the paying public, there was a queen to please. She must have been something of an incentive, because that most literate patroness of the arts was not without discriminating taste. She is known to have asked for Shakespeare's plays to be brought to her castle on various occasions, and the currying of her favors is hardly a thing Shakespeare would have spurned. He may have, as is generally believed, written one or more of his plays specifically on royal command. Such an assignment certainly would have stimulated growth.

There are still other and perhaps more subtle signs of maturation. One indication of a mind in process of development is a knack of adjusting to new circumstances. Involved in such a knack is an ability to anticipate, to guess, with some degree of accuracy, what is on the opposite side of the bridge before the bridge is crossed. An excellent example of just such anticipation occurred on the opening night of the new theatre Shakespeare and his company built, called The Globe.

Shakespeare wrote a new play for the occasion. It was *The Life of King Henry V.* A new play for a new theatre! Very fitting! But Shakespeare anticipated a problem. With uncanny awareness that the playgoers might find the new setting unfamiliar and therefore possibly upsetting, he wrote a prologue well calculated to deflate any and all complaints.

That prologue, which has become almost as famous as The Globe itself, was a twice-blessed masterpiece. It forestalled negative reactions due to inadequacies, and it set the stage in the imagination of the audience.

PROLOGUE

Enter Chorus

CHORUS. O for a Muse of fire, that would ascend
The brightest heaven of invention!
A kingdom for a stage, princes to act
And monarchs to behold the swelling scene!
Then should the warlike Harry, like himself,
Assume the port of Mars; and at his heels,
Leashed in like hounds, should famine, sword and fire
Crouch for employment. But pardon, gentles all,
The flat unraised spirits that have dared
On this unworthy scaffold to bring forth
So great an object. Can this cockpit hold
The vasty fields of France? Or may we cram
Within this wooden O the very casques
That did affright the air at Agincourt?
O, pardon! since a crooked figure may
Attest in little place a million;
And let us, ciphers to this great accompt,
On your imaginary forces work.
Suppose within the girdle of these walls
Are now confined two mighty monarchies,
Whose high upreared and abutting fronts
The perilous narrow ocean parts asunder.
Piece out our imperfections with your thoughts—
Into a thousand parts divide one man,
And make imaginary puissance;
Think, when we talk of horses, that you see them
Printing their proud hoofs i' the receiving earth—
For 'tis your thoughts that now must deck our kings,
Carry them here and there, jumping o'er times,

> Turning the accomplishment of many years
> Into an hour-glass. For the which supply,
> Admit me Chorus to this history,
> Who prologue-like your humble patience pray,
> Gently to hear, kindly to judge, our play.

If these few clues reveal a hint or two of how Shakespeare got to be the genius that he was, they are but asteroids in the universe of his creation. He no doubt did make a conscious effort to improve, yet in so doing he seemed to tower above the judgment of his time. He towers still above our judgment. Read him, see him, perform him, and direct him, we cannot possess him. On the contrary, he continues to possess us. We cannot profess to fully understand him, but we cannot fail to feel him. He masters our feelings to the extent that everything about him seems superior. Few can claim kinship to his genius. Yet, because he converts everything into excellence, few can resist his challenge to excellence.

If by some mystery still unrevealed to mortals, the gentle Will is watching, would the troubled world we know distress, bewilder, or intrigue him? No doubt he would view us much as he viewed his troubled world, with a kind of compassionate objectivity, a concern uncluttered with prejudice, a faith though unpreached, unruffled by fear, timidity, and hostility. No wonder philosophers call him philosopher, statesmen call him statesman, musicians call him musician.

Catholics think of him as Catholic, Protestants think of him as Protestant, atheists feel he champions atheism, skeptics see him as skeptic, and psychologists marvel at his psychology.

If Dante was the melodious priest of medieval Catholicism, perhaps we should, with Carlisle, call Shakespeare "The still more melodious priest of a true catholicism, the universal church of the future and of all times." Free of superstition, intolerance, fanaticism, and perversion, he seemed to have a god's-eye view of things, and with that view he could affirm humanity and all nature. Come, gentle Will. We need again such affirmation.

The cry is in the hearts of millions now, the cry to make a better world. Survival and a better world are common themes. "To be or not to be" is pertinent to the human race. The threat of ending for all mankind "the thousand natural shocks that flesh is heir to" does make Hamlets of us all. Survival! "Whether 'tis nobler in the mind to suffer the flings and arrows of outrageous fortune, or to take arms against a sea of troubles, and by opposing end them," is a quandary much too universal.

But should the race of man end its presence on this once-green earth, there would, alas, be no Horatio to tell our story, a thought too terrifying to face. Even the thought that there would be no telling of the Hamlet tale, no telling ever again, of any of the tales of Shakespeare's immortal men and women, is almost too dismal to contemplate. The alternative, then, is to make a world that can survive.

Help us, you men and women of Shakespeare's eternal world. You, with all your faults and foibles, with all your violences and virtues, with all your visions, dreams, ideals, with all your living and your dying, you all have things to tell us all. "O brave new world, that hath such people in it."

If we can still learn from history, and can learn history from Shakespeare, we may yet survive to make history. In a thousand years, or in a century, or even a generation hence, the fact that we have passed this way will not be without some influence.

When the water was put to boil for the midwifing of

Mary Shakespeare's baby, did the people of England pause, or did the queen declare a national holiday? Did even the farmers down the road suspend spring ploughing? No, nobody could possibly have known that the infant, squawling on the heated blanket, would one day change the course of cultural history, change it not with the sword, but with the word; change it not by conquest, but by compassion; change it by moving the hearts and minds of men and women there in his native England, and thence through time to come, around the globe.

Atlas, with the world on his shoulders, was the first insignia of The Globe theatre. Could the manager who hung that sign, or any of the people who saw it, have dreamed of its eventual significance? No, no more than they could have guessed that The Globe's first playwright would eventually encircle the globe with his plays, or that that playwright would draw to his plays the people of the world. No one could have guessed, either, that a time would come when restless citizens of earth would find in his plays some hints to help them in their crucial efforts to make a new world.

So, gentle Will, if you are still watching, give us your benison, or at least a wink. Thank you, Will. We will carry on.